Ideology and S▸

Ideology and Superstructure

in Historical Materialism

FRANZ JAKUBOWSKI
Introduction by Frank Furedi

Translated by Anne Booth

PLUTO PRESS
London • Winchester, Mass

This edition first published 1990 by
Pluto Press, 345 Archway Road, London N6 5AA
and 8 Winchester Place, Winchester
MA 01890, USA

First published in Great Britain 1976, reprinted 1978

British Library Cataloguing in Publication Data
Jakubowski, Franz
    Ideology and superstructure in historical materialism.
    1. Marxism. historical materialism
    I. Title
    335.4'119

    ISBN 0-7453-0389-7

Printed in Great Britain by Billing and Sons Ltd, Worcester

Contents

Introduction by Frank Furedi   vii
Franz Jakubowski: an introductory note   xxxv

CONSCIOUSNESS AND BEING
I   Marx and Engels on their predecessors
       The Critique of Hegelian Idealism   13
       The Critique of Feuerbach's Materialism   21

II   The Marxian problematic of base and superstructure
       Base   30
       Superstructure   37
       The Dialectical Relationship   58

III Distortion and renewal by Marx's followers
       The Distortion of the Question by the Epigones   66
       The Beginnings of Renewal   75

FALSE AND CORRECT CONSCIOUSNESS
IV   Alienation and reification
       The Self-alienation of Man and Commodity
       Fetishism   83
       Reification in Base and Superstructure   90

V   Ideology
       Ideology and the Concept of the Concrete
       Totality   98
       Ideology and the Classes of Bourgeois Society   104

VI   Proletarian class consciousness
       The Proletariat as Subject-Object in Capitalism   112
       Class Ideology and Class Consciousness   116
       Marxism as Ideology and as Humanism   123

Notes   129

Index   131

Introduction
FRANK FUREDI

Restating the Problem

There seems to be no end to the stream of commentaries on Marx
and interpretations of Marxism. Unfortunately few of the authors
of these works are concerned to develop Marxist theory. Instead
they focus narrowly on attempting to clarify Marx's views on
their particular sphere of interest and rarely go beyond the level
of textual analysis. Commentators often select a few paragraphs
from Marx's writings and treat these as the sum total of his
theory. This vulgar approach is particularly apparent in books
that purport to introduce Marx to the new reader. For example,
introductions targeted at students often quote briefly from the
Communist Manifesto, suggesting that key passages from this early
agitational pamphlet provide an adequate summary of the whole
of Marxist theory. More specialist texts treat the few pages of the
Preface to *A Contribution to the Critique of Political Economy* as a
complete statement of Marx's method of analysis.

Generations of interpreters of Marx have taken the brief comments on method in the 1857 Preface as a grand statement of the
Marxist world view. This approach has enabled them to proceed
effortlessly to the conclusion that Marxism provides inadequate
conceptual tools for those seriously concerned to understand
modern history and society in all their complexity. Indeed this
method of argument has so successfully exposed Marx's woeful
theoretical inadequacies that one wonders why it is necessary for
new authors continually to repeat it. It is striking that more than
50 years ago Jakubowski was already so familiar with the use of
the Preface to confuse and discredit Marxism that he announced
early in his book his intention to challenge this approach:
'Nothing has obscured our understanding of Marx's problematic
more than the habit which both Marxists and critics of Marx
make of quoting one paragraph from the Preface to *A Contribution
to the Critique of Political Economy*.'[1]

To readers who are familiar with Marx's 1857 Preface, which includes what is widely regarded as the most definitive statement of his method of analysis, Jakubowski's reservations may seem idiosyncratic. The key passage certainly seems a clear and boldly stated summary of Marx's approach to the study of history:

> In the social production of their existence, men invariably enter into definite relations, which are independent of their will, namely relations of production appropriate to a given stage in the development of their material forces of production. The totality of these relations of production constitutes the economic structure of society, the real foundation on which arises a legal and political superstructure and to which correspond definite forms of social consciousness. The mode of production of material life conditions the general process of social, political and intellectual life. It is not the consciousness of men that determines their existence, but their social existence that determines their consciousness.[2]

Some of the central concepts of Marxist theory – relations of production, forces of production, mode of production and superstructure – are discussed here in their inter-relationships for the first time. The proposition that social existence determines human consciousness is indeed a key theme in Marx's theory of history and society. What then is the objection to the use of this text by those who seek to explain the Marxist method?

Jakubowski objected to the way a few sentences from the Preface were widely interpreted as a summary of Marx's theory of historical materialism. He regarded the Preface as an outline of some of the conclusions arrived at through the theoretical work presented in the main body of the text. He criticised, not the use of the above quotation as such, but the way this brief statement of principles was treated as if it were the whole theory of historical materialism. The tendency to confuse the results of Marx's theory with the theory itself continues to this day. It is evident in the modern trend in commentaries on Marx to isolate key concepts, such as base and superstructure or forces and relations of production, and to discuss them without regard to the totality of the analysis from which they are derived. Many of the recent controversies in academic Marxism are really arguments about how to define these concepts. Questions such as 'What is included in the base?', 'How does the base determine the super-structure?', 'How do relations of production affect productive forces?' all assume that there is some fixed logic linking these concepts that it is the task of theory to elaborate and criticise.

As Jakubowski observed, both enemies and friends of Marxism adopt a similar procedure in attempting to explain his theoretical approach. Taking the Preface as the whole of historical materialism, those hostile to Marxism resort to the simple expedient of subjecting this provisional conceptual framework to heavy bombardment with empirical facts. When a certain fact appears to contradict the concept, Marx's theory is declared refuted. 'How is an ideology like Islamic fundamentalism or a phenomenon like child abuse determined by the economic base of capitalist society?', 'If capitalist social relations fetter the productive forces, how can you explain the expansion of the world economy and the development of technology over the past 50 years?', 'If politics is determined by economics, why are there vastly different forms of government in different capitalist countries?' – these are the sort of arguments that can be deployed with devastating effect against the straw-man Marxism derived from the above quotation from the Preface.

Among those more sympathetic to Marxism, the reduction of Marxist theory to the formulations of the Preface has led to the interminable 'base-superstructure' debate of recent years. The defect of the definitional approach shared by all protagonists in this debate is that it assumes that there is a fixed relationship between these concepts. All sides accept the premise that Marxist theory can be treated as a model that can be applied or refuted according to the prejudices of the author. In the course of the debate the origins of the key concepts concerned in the development of Marx's analysis of modern capitalist society are obscured. Yet the conclusions outlined in the Preface did not emerge out of thin air. For example, the proposition that it is 'not the consciousness of men that determines their existence, but their existence that determines their consciousness' was the result of a critical re-examination of Hegel's philosophy of law in the context of the role of legal processes in contemporary society.

By its very nature a critique tackles a specific form of thought in its particular social and historical context. However, the conclusions of a critique by no means exhaust the insights that can be provided by the methods of historical materialism. The aim of Marx's critique of Hegel was to derive ideological and legal notions from basic economic relations. Yet this approach provided only one side of the story since it could not explain how these ideological and legal notions evolved in modern society. This problem was tackled in Marx's major work, *Capital*, significantly subtitled *A Critique of Political Economy*. Without a consideration of the critique from which the Preface was derived, terms like base and superstructure become empty words embodying concepts of little value. Abstracted from their origins, they can be assigned any meaning and can be defined and re-defined according to the preoccupations of the author. Jakubowski's book proclaims its usefulness to Marxist theory by challenging from the outset those who would reduce it to an abstract schema.

The project of transforming Marxism into a model or a series of definitions is antithetical to the spirit of historical materialism. From its inception Marx's theory developed through a critique of the static approach of bourgeois social science which attempts to understand the world through defining and classifying phenomena. For Marxism, society is in a constant state of flux and particular phenomena can only be understood in their relationship and interaction with other phenomena in society. It is significant that Marx never once attempted to define key concepts such as commodity, capital, or capitalist. Others may seek to define a capitalist as a rich person or as an individual with particular skills in business, manufacture or commerce. For Marx, however, an individual became a capitalist only through establishing a relationship of exploitation with workers. Only through this relationship can the potential for wealth to be transformed into capital be realised. Marx was not concerned to define social phenomena, but to specify the *conditions* for their existence. In the absence of the precondition provided by the wage labour-capital relationship, a rich person may remain rich, but he will not become a capitalist.

Defining a social phenomenon takes it out of history and the social relationships within which it develops. Thus the phenomenon can no longer be situated within its relations to other phenomena or the wider totality. Yet comprehension of a phenomenon develops only through an understanding of its role in the totality within which it belongs. The concept of *totality* is central to Marxist theory, for if we are to understand an object it is necessary to examine all of its relations, connections and mediations to others. This is why the static definitional approach characteristic of bourgeois social science is so inadequate in the analysis of a dynamic society. As Grossman pointed out, social phenomena 'have no "fixed" or "eternal" elements or character, but are subject to constant change. A definition fixes the superficial attributes of a theory at any given moment or period, and thus transforms these attributes into something permanent and unchanging.'[3] Marx's method provides a dynamic approach, one which emphasises interaction, social process and movement. Marxist concepts develop through history: Marx insisted that phenomena should be studied in the process of movement and self-development.

Given that bourgeois social theory is based on the notion that facts are self-evident truths which can be understood and classified without studying their history, it is not surprising that non-Marxist writers should try to interpret Marxism in terms of definitions. It is however inexcusable for those who claim to stand in the Marxist tradition to adopt the definitional approach. Nobody who has studied Marx's *Capital* can be in any doubt about Marx's contempt for those who reduced science to the classification of hard facts and rigid definitions. In *Capital* he ridiculed those who took familiar concepts as the point of departure for their investigations. He dismissed as 'vulgar economy' the sort of theory that 'ruminates without ceasing on the materials long since provided by scientific economy, and there seeks explanations of the most obtrusive phenomena' and 'confines itself to systematising in a pedantic way'.[4]

Pursuing a similar line of attack, Marx challenged the quest of Proudhon and other utopian socialists for a ready-made model which only needed to be applied to reality. He accused them of 'hunting for a so-called "science" by means of which they want to devise a priori a formula for the "solution of the social question", instead of deriving their science from a critical knowledge of the historical movement'.[5] In the same vein Engels objected to those who attempted to use Marxist concepts as a rigid analytic framework. He insisted that

> all history must be studied afresh, the condition of existence of the different formations of society must be examined in detail before the attempt is made to deduce from them the political, civil law, aesthetic, philosophic, religious, etc, views responding to them.[6]

Engels repeatedly emphasised that historical materialism was a guide to social investigation rather than a system of concepts which could be mechanically imposed on society. He warned that 'the materialist method turns into its opposite if it is not taken as one's guiding principle in historical investigation but as a ready-made pattern according to which one shapes the facts of history to suit oneself.'[7]

The central methodological defect of the model-building interpretation of Marxism is that it inevitably endows abstract concepts with a reality they do not possess. Instead of studying the real movement of society, the model-builders are preoccupied with trying to fit reality into their conceptual framework. The contemporary movement known as Analytic Marxism is the most extreme expression of this trend. By incorporating the techniques of formal logic into Marxism, the Analytic Marxists rob historical materialism of its social content and transform it into a schema which purports to explain social phenomena in quantitative terms. As an illustration of the banality to which this approach reduces Marx's concepts, one leading Analytic Marxist writes that 'there is a set of social phenomena that does not fit into the traditional Marxist categories, such as base and superstructure. They include family life, education, social mobility, leisure activities, the distribution of mental and physical health, crime, etc.'[8]

In fact, from the standpoint of historical materialism no social phenomena fit into Marxist categories. The widespread use of phrases such as 'the traditional Marxist model of "base and super-structure"' is alien to Marxist theory.[9] Jakubowski challenged the tendency to abstract terms like base and superstructure, insisting that these are broad and indeterminate concepts. He argued that the 'unity of social life is so strong' that the only possible distinction between base and superstructure was a 'methodological one, for the purpose of throwing light on any one of the fundamental relationships'.[10] This interpretation stands in sharp contrast to the general tendency of academic Marxists to regard base and superstructure as categories corresponding directly to social reality.

The writings of the Analytic Marxist G.A.Cohen provide a particularly clear illustration of the widespread failure to grasp the limited analytic status of terms like base and superstructure. Cohen is constantly preoccupied with the difficulties of deciding what can be fitted into these categories:

> I now believe that, when we think about the superstructure, our fundamental concept should be a superstructural fact or phenomenon rather than that of a superstructural institution ... This move is motivated by a desire to avoid the unnecessary puzzlement that comes from asking questions like: do universities belong to the superstructure?[11]

The question of where universities fit in Cohen's model is no more absurd than the problem of what constitutes a 'superstructural fact'. It is the very distinction he draws between base and superstructure for the purpose of distinguishing between different spheres of social reality that is the core of the problem. From this perspective, Harman's argument that 'the distinction between base and superstructure is a distinction between social relations which are subject to immediate changes with changes in the productive forces, and those which are relatively static and resistant to change' simply reproduces the problem in a different form. While Harman and Cohen may disagree about how to draw the distinction between base and superstructure, they both assume that this process of establishing the content of polarised categories is useful in trying to understand the world.[12]

One of Jakubowski's most significant contributions was his critique of the mechanical counterposition of Marxist concepts. Following Marx's dictum that 'thought and being are indeed *distinct*, but they are also in unity with one another', he emphasised that each of these two elements acquired its meaning through its relationship with the other. In contrast to the dualistic, either/or outlook of the model-builders, Jakubowski insisted on the unity of subject and object, to the point where even their distinctiveness is acquired in their inter-relationship. The formal approach of academic commentators, and many of their radical critics, ruptures this dialectical whole and is thus incapable of grasping the real movement of society.

Jakubowski's critique of dualism was motivated by a desire to break out of the constraints imposed by the formalism of static interpretations of Marxism. In a key passage he emphasised the importance of the dialectical method that Marx and Engels took over from Hegel:

> Marx and Engels recognised the fruitful and revolutionary character of Hegel's philosophy as the fact that it dissolved the rigid definitiveness with which all previous philosophy had treated the results of human thought and action. A new concept appeared, of unending historical development.[13]

In a society in a constant process of change, nothing is definite or fixed. All social phenomena change and acquire new meaning in their constant interaction with other phenomena. Social phenomena do not have a rigidly defined 'essence' which can be expressed in static concepts. The 'essence' of social phenomena is only as durable as the relationships within which they exist. We can illustrate this point by paraphrasing Marx. An object with four legs which is a chair in one social situation becomes a throne in another. Whether it is a chair or a throne is determined, not by its inner essence, but by the social relationships within which it is placed.

Once the relationship between concepts and reality is understood from a historical perspective it is evident that fixed definitions are of little value. No real insights can be gained from philosophical speculation on the relationship between base and superstructure. As Jakubowski noted, 'any analysis of the extent to which ideological and material relationships interpenetrate must be made individually, according to each particular case.'[14]

For Marx, the question of how the base determines the superstructure could never arise, because this question presupposes the separation of two autonomous spheres of social reality. Historical materialism begins from the interconnectedness of social reality and social relationships. It denies the existence of fixed direct relationships between base and superstructure, or between being and consciousness, and seeks instead to grasp the dynamic of these relationships through the study of the historical development of society.

Historical Specificity

Whereas Analytic Marxists treat the relationship between base and superstructure as given, vulgar materialists emphasise the base side of the relationship and reduce ideological and political phenomena to what they call 'economics'. This approach reduces Marx's argument that the 'mode of production of material life conditions the general process of social, political and intellectual life' to the crass proposition that economic interests are the only motivation of human behaviour.

From the perspective of historical materialism, human consciousness is not the simple reflex of material life. Indeed such a mechanical interpretation of social phenomena has more in common with bourgeois sociology than with Marxism. For Marxism, the human subject does not sit outside the world passively experiencing its impact, but exists in a dynamic process of interaction with society. As Jakubowski put it, 'consciousness no longer stands outside being and is no longer separated from its object. It is a moving and moved part of the historical becoming of reality.'[15] Consciousness is part of reality and changes through changing reality. Lenin emphasised the same point, writing that 'consciousness not only reflects the objective world, it also creates it.'[16] The transformative potential of consciousness is a significant element in the making of history.

Once the historically relative status of facts is recognised, the whole project of model-building Marxism is immediately called into question. Because history cannot be reduced to a series of immutable facts, or a linear process of stages to a defined goal, a theory which is itself complete can be of little use in analysing the continual movement of social development. Thus Marxist theory must itself remain open-ended and its concepts ready to adapt to change. As Trotsky acutely observed, the *concept* 'is not a closed circle, but a loop, one end of which moves into the past, the other – into the future.'[17]

The view that theory arrives after the event to study a finished history is characteristic of the vulgar materialist caricature of Marxism popularised within the Stalinist movement from the 1930s onwards. However, with the declining influence of Stalinism in recent decades, traditional vulgar materialism and its one-sided emphasis on economic determination have given way to an equally one-sided idealist outlook. For today's academic Marxists economic life determines nothing and ideology and politics are everything in an inverted version of the materialist schema. It is ironic that the assumption that Marxism provides a suitably complete framework for the study of society is common to both schools, despite their quite different preoccupations.

Now that the idealist outlook is in the ascendant in the world of academic Marxism it is fashionable to criticise Marx as a vulgar economic reductionist who gave insufficient attention to matters of ideology and politics, culture and art. These criticisms of Marx are founded on the premises that superstructural phenomena exist more or less autonomously from material reality and that it is simplistic to argue that they are determined in any way by specific relations of production. Although most writers from the idealist school are bitterly hostile to vulgar materialism, they have much in common when it comes to the study of history. By 'freeing' the superstructure from the base, they are forced to consider the former outside the realm of historical change.

Idealist critics of Marx reject the dialectic of change and transformation that is at the core of the relationship between being and consciousness. Instead they assume that there is a series of eternal and immutable forces standing outside history which are independent of the influence of changing social reality. In recent years proponents of these idealist views have begun to adopt the almost metaphysical conviction that different ideologies and human identities have an inner dynamic of their own. Thus prejudices like sexism and racism are explained as permanent features of the human psyche. The most consistent advocate of this extreme idealist outlook is the French philosopher Louis Althusser, who proclaims baldly that 'ideology has no history', insisting that it exists independently of specific social circumstances. Instead of developing an analysis of ideology which is historically specific, Althusser proposes a 'theory of ideology in general'.[18]

Althusser's approach is to break Marxism into fragments and then to rebuild his own system of isolated static concepts assembled in a rigid structure which lacks any capacity to reflect the dynamic of modern society. Despite the grave defects of this theory, it remains, in diverse modified forms, the dominant influence in Western academic Marxism today. Thus Cohen, despite his subjectively antagonistic attitude towards Althusser, simply replaces his theory of ideology with a general theory of human needs:

> I claim, then, there is a human need to which Marxist observation is commonly blind ... It is the need to be able to say not what I can do but who I am, satisfaction of which has historically been found in identification with others in a shared culture based on nationality, or race, or religion or some slice or amalgam thereof.[19]

Cohen's observation that the need for self-identity is an eternal human need that must be studied in its own terms stands in sharp contrast to the Marxist approach to history. From a Marxist perspective, the need for self-identity, like any other social phenomenon, is not a self-evident fact. The problem of individual identity only emerged in particular historical circumstances. It did not exist, for example, in feudal communities in which an individual's position in a clearly defined social hierarchy was determined at birth. It is unlikely that either the lord of the manor or his serfs were unduly preoccupied with questions like 'who am I?'. It was only with the development of capitalism, the break-up of such rigidly ordered communities and the emergence of a society of atomised individuals united only through the market, that questions of individual identity could begin to arise.

Contrary to Cohen's assertion that self-identity is a universal human need, dialectical materialism regards it as a historically specific social phenomenon. Even with the emergence of the individual in modern society, the problem of identity cannot be reduced to the level of individual need. Identities are constructed through society and the identification of individuals with particular collectivities – as English or Scottish, black or white, male or female, Catholic or Protestant, gay or straight, Labour or Tory, militant or strikebreaker. The relative intensities and social significance of these identifications are in a constant state of flux according to diverse social and historical factors.

The question of identity or any other social phenomenon cannot be understood outside the process of historical development. Rather than trying to establish the terms of the relationship between base and superstructure or any other categories in *general*, Marx sought to examine each particular social relation *in its specificity* and in all its forms. Take for example his remarks on art:

> To examine the connection between spiritual production and material production it is above all necessary to grasp the latter itself not as a general category but in *definite* historical form ... If material production itself is not conceived in its *specific historical* form, it is impossible to understand what is specific in the spiritual production corresponding to it and the reciprocal influence of one on the other.[20]

For Marx it was necessary that both the forms of material production and those of artistic endeavour should be studied in their historical context. The relationship between the two could not be taken as given simply by asserting 'the reciprocal influence of one on the other'.

Marx emphasised that it was necessary to examine both the specific *art form* and the material conditions within which it emerged. He did not suggest that a specific art form could be explained simply by studying the sphere of production in the society from which it arose. Neither did he argue that art could be understood entirely on its own terms, independently from the prevailing relations of production. Works of art produced in one historical period may be appreciated in another era. However, to understand how a particular work originated it is necessary to study the relations of production of the society within which it was produced. Greek drama may be enjoyed, but not produced, in modern capitalist society. To understand why the tragedies of classical antiquity can still move human beings in the late twentieth century it is necessary to study both the specific forms of Greek drama and the specific material conditions of modern society. The exploration of the origins of a Greek play and the study of its contemporary impact cannot be achieved through the same analysis.

Marx was not interested in working out a theory of the development of art in general. His concern was to study the changing specific relations between art and the material conditions of production in determinate forms of society. His concepts were developed in the course of this analysis and in the process of social change were continually tested and modified. This is why Marx's analytic concepts lack the definite precision demanded by today's academic model-builders.

In their quest for fixed, sharply-defined concepts, academic Marxists are inevitably ill-at-ease with the indeterminate character of Marx's historical materialism. Callinicos' attempt to reconcile historical materialism with Analytic Marxism founders as a consequence of his formalistic approach:

> The fundamental concept of historical materialism is, in any case, that of mode of production. To specify the character of a mode of production is to give an account of the specific combination of the forces and relations of production it involves. There has been much discussion of these concepts in recent years, as a result of the attempts by Althusser and by Cohen to reconstruct a coherent theory of historical materialism from Marx's own evolving and often economistic usage.[21]

Callinicos' concern to turn Marxism into a 'coherent theory' leads to a misguided preoccupation with the formalisation of evolving concepts. What is fundamental about historical materialism is not any particular concept like mode of production, but the principle of *historical specificity*. It is the recognition of the historically relative character of social forms and hence the inevitably transient character of social relations that makes Marx's historicism so distinctive.

xix

What Callinicos disparages as Marx's 'evolving and often inconsistent usage' of concepts like forces and relations of production was no theoretical deficiency but a characteristic feature of the method of historical materialism. Unlike today's academic Marxists, Marx himself was far from certain about giving an account of 'the specific combination of the forces and relations of production'. He explicitly issued a warning 'not to be forgotten', that *the dialectic of the concepts productive force (means of production) and relations of production* was 'a dialectic whose boundaries are to be determined'.[22] Marx's lack of confidence about fixing the boundaries between concepts was not the result of a theoretical diffidence which can be overcome by the scholastic rigour of a Cohen or a Callinicos.

Marx was not concerned about formalising concepts, but with the specific relationships between relations of production and particular social forms. Following the comments quoted above he proceeded to a consideration of the ideology of law, noting that the 'really difficult point to discuss here is how the relations of production develop unevenly as legal relations'.[23] Marx's constant focus was not so much on concepts, as on the *relationships* between them, between form and content, subject and object, base and superstructure, in their historical development. One of the great merits of Jakubowski's book is the way that he rigorously reconstructed this approach. As he noted, the 'relation between consciousness and being can thus only be understood if being is conceived of dynamically as process.'[24]

Marx's most significant theoretical achievement was to clarify the historically specific character of social phenomena. The object of his scientific inquiry was to show how different social determinations interacted in specific circumstances. The indeterminate character of the boundaries between Marx's concepts was not the result of his personal theoretical idiosyncrasies, but the outcome of the constantly shifting nature of social reality itself. Only a theory oriented towards the historical movement of society is capable of identifying with any accuracy such conceptual boundaries, and then only in relation to the analysis of the particular subject under investigation. In this way historical materialism provides scope for the theoretical imagination; it cultivates the spirit of questioning and challenges the dull certitudes of conventional wisdom.

Theory and Practice

The mechanical counterposition of concepts like base and super-structure and the cult of model-building are the logical outcome of the contemplative approach of academic Marxism. The sharpest counterposition of all for this school is that between theory and reality. For academic Marxism, theory explains but does not touch real human relations. Lacking any experience of active intervention in society, academic theory yields only the wisdom of hindsight.

For Marxism, history is human history, made through the inter-action of the human subject with objective forces. Because Marxists recognise the constant movement of history it does not mean that they believe that historical change takes place automatically. Even when a particular society is ripe for change the active intervention of the subjective factor is necessary to realise this potential. This is why Marx constantly emphasised the unity of theory and practice in his discussion of the relations between subject and object. History is realised through the class struggle; under capitalism the subjective bearer of change is the working class. The participation of the subject in the making of history is not an arbitrary matter, but the result of the pressures of objective factors.

Marx's oft-quoted remark that 'men make their own history, but they do not make it as they please: they do not make it under circumstances chosen by themselves but under circumstances encountered, given, transmitted from the past' helps to elucidate the relation between subject and object. For the purposes of the present discussion it is necessary to emphasise the active side of the relationship, the fact that human beings 'make their own history'. The development of conscious thought, which is in part the result of the theoretical analysis of the movement of society, becomes another objective precondition for historical change.

Contemplative philosophy in both its bourgeois and model-building forms one-sidedly conceives of humanity and human action as the product of social forces. Of course Marx too recog-nised that forms of consciousness and behaviour were socially determined. However, this is not at all a distinctively Marxist view. Earlier materialist philosophers from Montesquieu to Feuerbach recognised that human beings were the product of the natural and social environment. Marx went far beyond the Enlightenment view that human beings were merely products of their circumstances with his insistence that the distinctive feature of humanity was its capacity to transform itself through its own intervention in the natural and social world. For Marxism, human consciousness develops through human activity in the world; it is a 'factor in changing social reality'.[25]

Marx's famous dictum that 'until now philosophers have only *interpreted* the world in various ways: the point however is to *change* it' sums up his dialectical appreciation of the relationship between theory and practice. The target of Marx's polemical attack on philosophers was not theory as such, but speculative theory of the type that still predominates in modern society. Marx never counterposed action to thought, but elaborated an approach in which action was assimilated to thought because thought was oriented towards action. Marx considered that it was impossible to understand society through mere speculation; only active intervention in the world could ensure the conscious appreciation of reality. Marxist theory does not develop in an arbitrary way in the heads of those who have been initiated in its texts. It can only develop in relation to the problems thrown up by history. The consciousness that emerges from the confrontation between human thought and social reality can potentially become an element in the transformation of that reality. Marxist theory is a means of endowing action with consciousness, which can then contribute to the development of a subjective factor capable of making history.

From the Marxist perspective the familiar radical exhortation to 'put your theory into practice' makes little sense. This approach assumes a theory which has already been worked out and only needs to be implemented. Drawing heavily from Hegel, Marx emphasised the continual process of historical development within which human thought and action were not mechanically separated, but interdependent elements. However, Marx criticised Hegel's idealist way of posing the unity of thought and action and his view that history was made in thought as the consciousness of philosophers:

Already in *Hegel* the *Absolute Spirit* of history has its material in the *Mass* and finds its appropriate expression in *philosophy*. The philosopher, however, is only the organ through which the maker of history, the Absolute Spirit, arrives at self-consciousness *retrospectively* after the movement has ended. The participation of the philosopher in history is reduced to this retrospective consciousness, for the real moment is accomplished by the Absolute Spirit unconsciously. Hence the philosopher appears on the scene *post-festum*.[26]

Whereas in Hegel's view human consciousness developed retrospectively, for Marx the human subject was no longer speculative and contemplative, but a practical agent of social transformation. Knowledge itself is not given but is appropriated through practice.

At a time when passive academic interpretations of Marxism are in the ascendant, Jakubowski's treatment of the relationship between theory and practice is supremely relevant. Jakubowski wrote that 'the man who knows reality no longer stands outside history like Hegel's "philosopher" but is himself a factor in transforming social relations. Theory no longer exists merely *post-festum* but becomes a lever in the revolutionary process.'[27] He insisted that activity, understanding, theorising and formulating new problems were all elements in the ceaseless process of social change, elements which could not be understood in isolation from one another and the whole movement of history. In capitalist society the separation of theory from practice is overcome through the conscious expression of the struggles of the working class. 'Theory becomes material power as soon as it seizes the masses', as Marx put it in 1844. The power of Marxist theory is derived, not from the elegance of its arguments, but from its capacity to make conscious the unconscious forces driving towards social change.

Jakubowski's project of re-establishing the revolutionary dynamic of Marxism began from his insistence on placing theory within history. The mechanical separation of Marxist concepts by the model-builders is the direct result of their remoteness from society. Once Marxism ceases to interact with society it ceases to be Marxism and it can become the plaything of professors concerned with schemas, models and formal definitions. Such academic Marxists hold dialectics in contempt because they seek to verify their theory by measuring it against the facts rather than by testing it in practice.

While Jakubowski dealt rigorously with many critical questions about the relationship between theory and practice, it is worth considering one problem that he did not directly address. As we have seen, Marxist theory develops through the class struggle which it endows with consciousness, and in this way the struggles of the working class provide the means for testing the adequacy of theory. For Marxists intervention in the class struggle is the equivalent of laboratory experimentation for natural scientists. History does not always provide the same scope for Marxist experimentation, however. Periods of struggle are followed by phases of relative stability and even conservatism. Thus Marxism inevitably develops unevenly in relation to the uneven experience of working-class struggle. This gives a historically relative character to the development of Marxist theory and class-consciousness. Periodic limits to social action act as a barrier to the development of consciousness.

Jakubowski's book is in many ways the product of a period in which the limits to theoretical experimentation were particularly tightly imposed. Written in 1936, at a time when the working class throughout Europe was in retreat before fascism, the book is a product of an era of proletarian defeat. It is a remarkable achievement that Jakubowski was able to go so far in giving expression to the liberatory impulse of Marxist theory in the darkest days of the twentieth century. Nevertheless, during the 1930s, Jakubowski could not go further than posing the right questions – the times were inhospitable towards those who attempted to implement new solutions.

Jakubowski's critical attitude towards Lenin should be understood in the context of the isolation and defeat of the Russian Revolution in the 1920s. In his book Jakubowski accused Lenin of adopting the dualistic approach characteristic of those who counterpose being to consciousness. This interpretation of Lenin's writings was perhaps understandable if his 1909 polemical pamphlet 'Materialism and Empirio-criticism' was taken as his major statement on the method of historical materialism. However, Lenin's later writings on these matters, collected in his *Philosophical Notebooks* (a work which was probably not available to Jakubowski) reveal a remarkably clear appreciation of the dialectical unity of theory and practice. In the *Notebooks* Lenin writes that 'man's consciousness not only reflects the objective world, but creates it' and adds that 'the practice of man and of mankind is the test, the criterion of the objectivity of cognition.'[28] Lenin's own reconstruction of the materialist dialectic and the relationship between theory and practice was in fact quite consistent with Jakubowski's approach.

Our concern here is not to defend Lenin's reputation, but to draw attention to the profound understanding of the relationship between theory and practice that emerged in the Bolshevik tradition. It is well known that Lenin's re-examination of Hegel's dialectical method between 1914 and 1916 was stimulated by the new problems that were thrown up for the working-class movement by the imperialist war that broke out in 1914. This turbulent period provided exceptional opportunities for experimentation and hence for the development of Marxist theory. The subsequent experience of proletarian revolution in Russia yielded unprecedented insights into the relationship between theory and practice.

Writing, like Jakubowski, in the grim 1930s, Trotsky too revealed the richness of the Bolshevik tradition in his own comments on the relation between theory and practice:

> Marxism considers itself to be the conscious expression of an unconscious historical process ... a process that coincides with its expression only at its very highest points, when the masses with elemental force smash down the doors of social routine and give victorious expression to the deepest needs of historical development. The highest theoretical consciousness of an epoch at such moments merges with the immediate action of the lowest oppressed masses who are the farthest away from theory. The creative union of consciousness with the unconscious is what we usually call inspiration. Revolution is the violent inspiration of history.[29]

Differing levels of consciousness among workers in different countries at different times cannot be explained by differing intellectual capacities, but only by the opportunities provided by history. The capacity to give consciousness to the historical process develops through the advance of the working class and its struggles.

But what happens in periods of 'social routine' when Marxist theory inevitably becomes remote from the day-to-day activities of workers? This question must have haunted Jakubowski as he fled from Nazi terror in his native Poland in the late 1930s. Today this question is also particularly relevant. Over the past 30 years, and especially in the 1980s, Marxism has come under a sustained ideological attack. Today, intellectual opinion East and West is intensely hostile to Marxism. The negative experience of Stalinist rule in the Soviet Union and Eastern Europe appears to provide irrefutable proof of the futility of revolutionary Marxism. The relative passivity of the Western working class over the past decade seems to call into question the traditional Marxist insistence on the revolutionary potential of the proletariat. The remoteness of Marxism from the experience of the working class is just as much a problem today as it was in the 1930s. Unfortunately, Jakubowski's attempt to tackle this problem is the most disappointing part of his book.

Class Consciousness

Jakubowski fiercely contested Lenin's theory of organisation. He challenged the well-known argument of Lenin's pamphlet 'What is to be Done?' that class-consciousness does not arise spontaneously from the struggles of the working class, but has to be introduced from without by the revolutionary party. There are three aspects to Jakubowski's critique of Lenin: (1) He accused Lenin of rupturing the unity of theory and practice by isolating theory from struggle; (2) He argued that Lenin's view that the proletariat by itself could generate only a trade-union consciousness was incomplete; (3) He insisted that Marxism was the unity of the two forms of consciousness that arise from the working class and hence did not need to be introduced from the outside.[30]

Let's look at Jakubowski's coherently argued points more closely.

Most objections to Lenin's statement about bringing theory into the working class from outside confuse the question of the *origin* of Marxist theory with its *development*. That Marxism originated outside the working class is a matter of fact not interpretation. However, whatever its origin, Marxism can only develop further together with class-consciousness through the struggles of the proletariat.

The real issue at stake is not the origin of Marxist theory but that of class-consciousness. Lenin argued that the working class could not on its own acquire class-consciousness, not because he believed that workers lacked intelligence, but simply because class-consciousness did not arise spontaneously. Nobody – whether worker, intellectual or capitalist – can become class-conscious spontaneously, on their own. The development of class-consciousness is restricted because of the limited character of the experience of any individual worker or any section of the working class.

Individuals or groups react to their conditions with the consciousness that arises from their particular experience. Lenin argued that trade-union consciousness was the spontaneous reaction of wage labourers in struggle, just as anarchism was the instinctive outlook of the angry petit-bourgeois. In the course of an industrial dispute workers in one section of industry or services go into conflict with a particular employer or group of employers. They question the terms – pay, hours and conditions – on which their employers exploit workers; they do not generally challenge the exploitative system of wage labour. The wage labour-capital relationship can lead to great outbursts of militancy, but it does not in itself result in the emergence of a movement for communist revolution. While militancy may threaten the employers and even challenge the state authorities, it rarely questions the system in its entirety.

Workers may take militant, even violent, action against their bosses and the police – and still not question the operation of the capitalist system from the perspective of the working class as a whole. Thus workers may be very militant – and still be pro-capitalist in their wider outlook, expressing, for example, backward prejudices against women and black people. Similar limitations on the development of consciousness are imposed on other sections of society. Thus Jews reacting against anti-Semitism may well identify gentiles in general as the problem;

blacks fighting the effects of racism may view all white people as the enemy; and many women blame their experience of discrimination simply on men. In all these cases such responses are an advance on passivity, but they express the limited awareness of the nature of oppression in capitalist society that inevitably results from generalising from a narrow range of personal experience.

The consciousness that develops in response to a specific experience of oppression does not in itself lead to a general understanding of society. Indeed, when the partial consciousness of any particular social group becomes consolidated, it may have divisive consequences. The ruling class has proved itself adept at manipulating sectional, racial and gender divisions to strengthen its grip over society.

Class-consciousness develops through a critique of the *totality* of capitalist social relations. It presupposes transcending the limitations of individual or sectional experience to achieve a wider awareness of the experience of society as a whole. The working class is uniquely placed to achieve this wider consciousness because the condition of its own liberation is the transcendence of society as a whole. Unlike other revolutionary classes in the past, the working class has no special privileges or sectional interests to protect: it has no form of property to preserve. By its very existence the working class is forced to work collectively and its position is determined by its collective strength. As individuals, or as isolated sections, workers remain at the mercy of the capitalist class. Attempts by particular employers to buy off sections of the working class by offering better pay and conditions are simply offers of better terms of exploitation, a gesture to make the reality of powerlessness more tolerable.

It is the absence of any objective special interests that endows the working class with the status of a universal class and the capacity to represent the interests of society as a whole. The working class needs not only to abolish exploitation, but also to abolish *itself* as a class through the overthrow of capitalist society. To achieve a more developed consciousness of its revolutionary potential under capitalism, it is essential that the working class broadens its challenge to the capitalist order from the sphere of its immediate economic concerns. This is why Lenin insisted that class-consciousness could not be restricted to trade unionism, but required a rejection of all forms of oppression.

Capitalism not only creates a collective working class but it also divides it into different sections according to occupation, skill, pay, etc., and different groupings according to nationality, race, gender, religion, etc. These divisions are consolidated by capitalist politics and ideology which emphasise an individual rather than a collective outlook on all important social issues. For respectable public opinion there is no such thing as class, but only individuals who identify themselves as family men, working mothers, British patriots, football supporters, churchgoers, animal-lovers. The politics of individualism influences workers and undermines their capacity to act as an independent class. Simple trade unionism does not offer an alternative to these wider ideological appeals. Working-class consciousness and politics require not just a rejection of the experience of wage labour but an alternative to the *entire system of bourgeois politics*.

No individual can transcend their own experience in isolation. It is only through organisation and collective activity, through the intervention of the revolutionary party, that fragmented and partial experiences can be synthesised into an outlook that approximates the general experience of society. The revolutionary party does stand outside the working class, but only to the extent necessary for individual revolutionaries to overcome the limitations of their narrow personal experience. The limits of sectional experience and the consciousness that corresponds to it provide the main impulse for Lenin's theory of organisation. To complete Jakubowski's discussion of theory and practice it is necessary to look at the question of organisation more closely. How does theory become practical theory and practice become conscious practice?

Theory does not automatically become practice. Lukacs suggested that if theory 'really intends to point the way to its own fulfilment in practice' it must develop an 'organisational arm'.[31] Theory without organisation is merely ideas without consequences. It is only through organisation that theory acquires a form through which it can be tested. Most of the time, the relation between theory and practice is only semi-conscious; organisation is necessary to make this relationship conscious. In his path-breaking study of the problem, Lukacs described organisation as 'the form of mediation between theory and practice'.[32] Through organisation, theory acquires the potential for acting on history. Once it is expressed through organisation, theory is forced to come to terms with itself through action, and class-consciousness can become a reality. Through the medium of the party the synthesis of diverse experiences can be reproduced as a total critique of capitalist society.

Class-consciousness remains an enduring problem because it is not something that is easily expressed. The basis of this consciousness is the experience and struggle of the working class. But, as with all such relations, the link between the class struggle and consciousness is not direct or automatic. By situating particular struggles within a wider totality people can go beyond gaining partial insights and acquire a wider consciousness from the point of view of the working class as a whole. Organisation provides the means for the transformation of insights into conscious experience.

Consciousness does not develop in a linear, cumulative, way but concretely in relation to specific experiences. The awareness developed in one phase of social development does not guarantee its relevance in another time and place – if it did, world revolution would have triumphed long ago. The lessons of historic battles do not remain fixed in the outlook of human beings. In periods of defeat past lessons and insights are suppressed by the urgent problems of the present. In the dull routine of life under stable capitalist rule the experience of collective struggle in the past provides no ready antidote to conservatism and passivity. Yet the experience of the past struggles remains an important resource for the reconstruction of class-consciousness. For example, the defeat of the first attempt at revolution in Russia in 1905 provided a vital input into the theory that clarified the role of the working class in the successful revolution of 1917. This is where organisation is so important. In periods of reaction revolutionary organisation is not immune to the pressures of isolation, conservatism and routine. But through providing a form through which theory is expressed, the party provides a medium through which the significance of experiences of the past can be assessed in relation to the problems of the present and the future. The working class is not spontaneously aware of its own history – that awareness is kept alive through the medium of the party.

The existing state of society imposes sharp limits on how far it is possible to clarify the problem of class-consciousness without mystifying it further. There are no intellectual solutions to the problem, only the possibility of acting, not in an individual random manner, but collectively, through organisation that gives action a conscious direction and can assimilate its results. Action provides the material for reflection and organisation appropriates the reflection, through providing a form for further action.

For anybody seriously concerned about the problems of class-consciousness today, Jakubowski's book is essential reading. His reconstruction of the tradition of Marxist humanism provides an important counterpoint to the contemplative commentaries that now pass for Marxism. His insistence that the role of the proletariat as the subjective bearer of social change can only be realised through the development of class-consciousness places him firmly in the revolutionary tradition. His emphasis on the principle of historical specificity is the key to breaking out of the straitjacket of formalism in which the academics have placed Marxist theory. If the re-publication of Jakubowski's work stimulates a wider recognition that the appropriate concern of Marxist theory is the problems thrown up by the unfolding of contemporary history, rather than sterile speculation about its own concepts, then it could make a significant contribution to the development of class-consciousness.

Frank Furedi
January 1990

Notes

1. F. Jakubowski, *Ideology and Superstructure in Historical Materialism* (London: Pluto Press, 1990) p. 14.
2. K. Marx, *A Contribution to the Critique of Political Economy* (Moscow: Progress Publishers, 1970) pp. 20–1.
3. H. Grossman, 'The evolutionist revolt against classical economics' in *The Journal of Political Economy*, Vol. 51, Nos 5 and 6, p. 517.

4. K. Marx, *Capital* Vol. 1 (London: Lawrence and Wishart, 1974) p. 85.
    Marx took great objection to his critic Wagner for suggesting that he derived use value and exchange value from the *'concept of value'*. He wrote, 'That is all babbling ... I do not proceed on the basis of "concepts".' See K. Marx, 'Notes on Wagner' in K. Marx, *Value Studies* (London: New Park, 1976) p. 214.
5. 'Marx to Schweitzer', 24 January 1863 in *Marx and Engels Selected Correspondence* (Moscow: Progress Publishers, 1975) p. 148.
6. 'Engels to Schmidt', 4 August 1890, in *Marx and Engels Selected Correspondence* (Moscow: Progress Publishers, 1975) p. 393.
7. 'Engels to Ernst', 5 June 1890, in *Marx and Engels Selected Correspondence* (Moscow: Progress Publishers, 1975).
8. J. Elster, *Making Sense of Marx* (Cambridge University Press, 1985) p. 34.
9. An example of the usage of this phrase is: T. Bottomore, *Sociology: A Guide to problems and literature* (London: Allen & Unwin, 1987) p. 53.
10. F. Jakubowski, *Ideology and Superstructure in Historical Materialism* (London: Pluto Press, 1990) p. 37.
11. G.A. Cohen, *History, Labour, and Freedom: Themes from Marx* (Oxford: Polity Press, 1988) p. 178.
12. C. Harman, 'Base and Superstructure' in *International Socialism*, Vol. 32, 1986, p. 2.
13. F. Jakubowski, *Ideology and Superstructure in Historical Materialism* (London: Pluto Press, 1990) p. 18.
14. F. Jakubowski, *Ideology and Superstructure in Historical Materialism* (London: Pluto Press, 1990) p. 38.
15. F. Jakubowski, *Ideology and Superstructure in Historical Materialism* (London: Pluto Press, 1990) p. 60.
16. V.I. Lenin, 'Philosophical Notebooks' in *Collected Works*, Vol. 38, (Moscow: Progress Publishers, 1972) p. 212.
17. L. Trotsky, *Trotsky's Notebooks, 1933–35. Writings on Lenin, Dialectics and Evolutionism* (New York: Columbia University Press, 1986) p. 78.
18. L. Althusser, *Lenin and Philosophy and Other Essays* (London: New Left Books, 1977) pp. 150, 152.
19. G.A. Cohen, *History, Labour, and Freedom: Themes from Marx* (Oxford: Polity Press, 1988) p. 140.
20. K. Marx, *Theories of Surplus Value Part I* (Moscow: Progress Publishers, 1968) p. 285.
21. A. Callinicos, *Making History: Agency, structure and change in social theory* (Oxford: Polity Press, 1989) p. 43.
22. K. Marx, *Grundrisse* (Harmondsworth: Penguin Books, 1973) p. 109.
23. K. Marx, *Grundrisse* (Harmondsworth: Penguin Books, 1973) p. 109.

24. F. Jakubowski, *Ideology and Superstructure in Historical Materialism* (London: Pluto Press, 1990) p. 60.
25. F. Jakubowski, *Ideology and Superstructure in Historical Materialism* (London: Pluto Press, 1990) p. 61.
26. K. Marx and F. Engels, 'The Holy Family' in K. Marx and F. Engels, *Collected Works*, Vol. 4 (London: Lawrence and Wishart, 1975) pp. 85–6.
27. F. Jakubowski, *Ideology and Superstructure in Historical Materialism* (London: Pluto Press, 1990) p. 61.
28. V.I. Lenin, 'Philosophical Notebooks' in *Collected Works*, Vol. 38, (Moscow: Progress Publishers, 1972) pp. 211–212.
29. Cited in L. Trotsky, *Trotsky's Notebooks, 1933–35* (New York: Columbia University Press, 1986) p. 70.
30. F. Jakubowski, *Ideology and Superstructure in Historical Materialism* (London: Pluto Press, 1990) p. 120.
31. G. Lukacs, *History and Class Consciousness* (London: Merlin Press, 1968) p. 299.
32. G. Lukacs, *History and Class Consciousness* (London: Merlin Press, 1968) p. 299.

FRANZ JAKUBOWSKI: AN INTRODUCTORY NOTE

Franz Jakubowski was born on 10 June 1912 in what is now Poznàn, in Poland, where his father was a doctor. He grew up in Danzig, which was then a "free city" under the League of Nations, a casualty of the Versailles Treaty suspended between Germany and Poland. Jakubowski attended the municipal school in Danzig, leaving in 1930, the year in which he also became attracted to marxism. Between 1930 and 1933 he was studying law in Heidelberg, Berlin, Munich and Wroclaw (Breslau) successively. At Wroclaw he joined the Socialist Workers' Party, a communist oppositionist group which was strong enough to produce a daily paper. His adherence to the trotskyist movement coincided with Hitler's accession to power.

In Easter 1933 he went to Basle University to complete his degree with studies in political science. There he came into contact with a recently arrived professor named Fritz Belleville, who at that time was both a national leader of the German trotskyist movement and a member of the Frankfurt School (in particular, he was a friend and disciple of Karl Korsch). Both men took part in an active group of revolutionary socialist students.

Jakubowski completed his studies in 1936 and returned to Danzig, where what was virtually a Nazi government had already taken over, tempered only by the presence of the League of Nations high commissioner. He soon became the spokesman of the trotskyist group in the city, which called itself the Spartacus League. The group was an active one: it worked amongst the Danzig dockers to black arms shipments to Franco, for example. It was also large enough to be taken seriously by the official communist party in the city, which in August 1936 offered to form a front with the group led by Jakubowski. The offer was quickly curtailed by the Moscow trials and the Comintern's sudden discovery that all communist oppositionists were in fact Gestapo agents.

This "discovery" was somewhat contradicted by the fact that in December 1936 the majority of the group, about sixty people, were arrested by the Nazi authorities. At the trial Jakubowski, as the "ringleader", was condemned to three years' imprisonment along with nine others (what the Nazis did with the rest is not known). Trotsky wrote at length on this trial; for the first time, he began to talk about the Soviet and Nazi prosecutors in equivalent terms. In the journal *Lutte Ouvrière* (no. 54, 27 August 1937), an ironic thread runs through, sketching out the similarities between the form and language of the Danzig trial and the Moscow show trials. Trotsky says sarcastically: "Jakubowski in particular was accused of having, in one article, 'compared the Moscow show trials with the trial of the Reichstag incendiaries'. The prosecutor (Hoffman, not Vyshinsky) was indignant at this strange comparison."

This same article finishes on a more explicit note: "The Fascist prosecutor did not accuse the Danzig trotskyists of terrorism, sabotage or espionage, and he did not ask for their heads. This can be explained by the fact that the totalitarian régime in Danzig is still young... Stalin would appear now to be the instructor of Fascism. The GPU gives lessons to the Gestapo." In spite of this relative "youth" of Fascism, however, the defendants needed a great deal of courage to state their convictions from the dock, as they did.

Jakubowski's family managed to secure his release on the grounds that he was not a citizen of Danzig (he was in fact a German citizen), and he travelled via Denmark and Cuba to the USA. At this point, according to Boris Fraenkel in the postscript to the French edition of this book, "the itinerary of the revolutionary theoretician (and the political individual), Franz Jakubowski, comes to a halt"; and Fraenkel supplies no more information. But an individual is political by his very existence, not according to his adherence to the workers' movement. The career of Wilhelm Reich, who made a similar journey as a refugee (and whom Jakubowski cited in his original bibliography), illustrates the point: even in moving to a bizarre rightwing position, Reich in fact carried on a kind of anarchic partisan warfare against McCarthyite America from the stockade of his paranoia. Jakubowski himself changed his name to Frank Fisher, and became one of the initiators of the Alexander Herzen Foundation. He died in 1970.

Ideology and Superstructure was published in Danzig under the title *Der ideologische Uberbau in der materialistischen Geschichtsauffassung*, in 1936, and was the outcome of Jakubowski's doctoral thesis. A remarkable product of the barren 1930s, it reaffirms the humanist tradition in marxism without ever losing sight of the practical exigencies of bitter struggle, a struggle which at the time when Jakubowski was writing had become a defensive one and had condemned marxist theory to a whole period of dogma and isolation from the workers' movement. From the gathering darkness, Jakubowski writes: "For historical materialism to live again and bear fruit, in its original humanist form, the working-class movement must again reach the level which it has reached before on a narrower base of capitalist development and the theory must again be the adequate expression of that movement" (p. 127): for us, at a time when mass class struggles are taking place against a capitalism that has undergone an unprecedented extension of its base, and when the underlying humanist tendencies in marxism are being deepened in fresh ways by a variety of thinkers, Franz Jakubowski's prediction is a reminder of the continuity between the best of the past and the new routes being dug by practice and theory today.

C. G.

CONSCIOUSNESS AND BEING

CHAPTER I: Marx and Engels on their Predecessors

The Critique of Hegelian Idealism

"Modern socialism", wrote Friedrich Engels, "is, in its content, primarily the product of the perception on the one hand of the class antagonisms existing in modern society between possessors and non-possessors, wage workers and bourgeois; and, on the other hand, of the anarchy ruling in production. In its theoretical form, however, it originally appears as a further and ostensibly more logical extension of the principles established by the great French philosophers of the eighteenth century. Like every new theory, it had at first to link itself to the intellectual material which lay ready at hand, however deep its roots lay in economic facts."[1]

If we are to examine the relation between consciousness and being in historical materialism, we must pay particular attention to the ideas which Marx and Engels already found in front of them. Lenin, the orthodox marxist, points out that in order to be able to understand Marx properly, "we have to organise a systematic study of Hegel, conducted from the point of view of materialism". Everyone, marxists and non-marxists alike, recognises that the dialectic is of fundamental importance to marxist theory. And whatever Marx's overall attitude towards Hegel, he always saw himself as Hegel's disciple and successor on this particular question of the dialectic.[2] Therefore we can only get a correct grasp of Marx's problematic if we look at it in the light of his divergence from Hegel.

At the same time, Marx's conception of historical materialism developed not only out of this but also out of the polemic against contemporary materialism as he found it, embodied by Ludwig Feuerbach. However, Feuerbach's writings had actually had a decisive influence on Marx's critique of hegelian idealism. "The enthusiasm was general: we were all Feuer-

13

bachians," wrote Engels, although the influence was not quite so great on Marx. As early as 1843, the year when Feuerbach's *Philosophy of the Future* appeared, Marx was already criticising Feuerbach in a letter to Ruge (13 March) for talking too much about nature and too little about politics. In *The Holy Family* however, written two years later in 1845, Marx was still emphasising Feuerbach's importance as the critic of hegelian philosophy, the thinker who brought it to a close. It is only in the *Theses on Feuerbach*, one of the essential sources of historical materialism, that he definitely distinguishes himself not only from the idealism of Hegel but also from all previous kinds of materialism, including Feuerbach.

Marx's own problematic springs from this dispute with Hegel and Feuerbach, whom he saw as the typical representatives of the idealist and materialist philosophies. Nothing has obscured our understanding of Marx's problematic more than the habit which both marxists and critics of Marx make of quoting one paragraph from the *Preface to "The Critique of Political Economy"* along with a few similar passages, while ignoring the question of where Marx and Engels found that problematic and how they developed it from that point. I shall attempt to avoid this mistake by basing the first part of the discussion mainly on their early writings.

"The basic question of all philosophy, particularly the new, concerns the relation between thought and being," wrote Engels in *Ludwig Feuerbach*. "If one accepts in a completely naturalistic way 'consciousness', 'thought' as something given, something at the outset in contrast to being, to nature, then it must seem extremely curious that consciousness and nature, thought and being, the laws of thought and the laws of nature, should bear such a close correspondence." This "curious correspondence" led the founders of the materialist conception of history, Marx and Engels, to reject any dualistic model of the relation between consciousness and being. Their point of departure is the *unity* of the two. This is so self-evident to them that no detailed defence of this position can be found anywhere in their writings; we only come across occasional remarks such as the one above. Of course, it must be admitted that in the early writings (*The Holy Family, The German Ideology*) thought is emphatically considered to depend on being. But this is because Marx and Engels are taking it for granted that the dualist, kantian version of this particular thesis has already been overcome.

As I shall demonstrate later, their "negligence" in this respect was quite justifiable. However, the result of it has been that historical materialism has suffered a multitude of distortions at the hands of their followers, let alone their opponents. Two mistakes have arisen which could surely have been avoided by a more careful study of Marx's and Engels's ideas on this question. One is the frequent accusation that Marx and Engels deny the reality of consciousness — an accusation which only appears to be well-founded if certain passages are quoted in isolation. The other consists of a regression into a pre-hegelian, undialectical opposition between consciousness and being — a mistake which can be found in the writings of Lenin and his followers. I shall deal with both of these later on. Meanwhile, in order to start out not just from the sense but from the words of Marx, I shall point out a sentence from the *Economic and Philosophical Manuscripts of 1844*: "Thought and being are indeed *distinct*, but they are also in unity with each other."

Of course I too am taking this sentence out of context, but it does show the dialectical character of Marx's thinking with unusual clarity: there is scarcely any other reference to be found concerning this particular problem. The reason for this is not difficult to discover. It is one of the points where the relationship with Hegel is most evident, and Marx and Engels explicitly recognise themselves as the disciples of Hegel in this respect — their own research and discoveries, they believe, can add nothing else. Hegel, for them, had already definitively overcome the kantian dualism between consciousness and being. "The decisive refutation of [Kant's] view has already been made by Hegel, so far as this is possible from the standpoint of idealism," wrote Engels. Marx considers the reference to Hegel to be enough, by itself, to prove the existence of a dialectical unity in explicit opposition to Kant. When he discusses the problem of form and content, for example, as early as 1843, he simply uses Hegel's formula to refute the kantian dualism:

15

"Form has no validity except as the form of its content."

But although in hegelian philosophy the contradiction between being and consciousness has already been transcended and transformed into a unity, this unity is only a unity within thought, i.e. a unity within only one of the two elements of the contradiction. Feuerbach pointed this out when he said that, for Hegel, "Thought is the subject, being the predicate," thus indicating that Hegel's "unity" is apparent, not real.

Engels made a sharp distinction between the *unity* of consciousness and being and the *identity* of consciousness and being. He saw the argument between idealism and materialism as no more than an argument about whether it is mind or nature that is primordial; he considered it necessary to go further and discuss the question of "identity", of whether thought is capable of knowing the *real* world.

> "With Hegel, for example, the affirmative answer to this question is self-evident; for what we perceive in the real world is, for him, precisely its thought-content, i.e. that which gradually turns the world into a realisation of the Absolute Idea . . . but it is obvious to anyone that thought is capable of knowing a content which, from the outset, is a thought-content."[3]

Hegel takes for granted the possibility of knowing truth and the correspondence between thought and being. He endows the Idea alone with reality — beyond the Idea there is no real being: "The Spiritual alone is the Real, the being-in-itself . . . it is in and for itself."

This *identity* of thought with being can only be asserted by eliminating one of the two elements (in this case, being); it prevents a real, dialectical *unity* between the two. "Logical laws are at the same time ontological laws . . . the basis of thought and of being is identical."[4] Being is refined into thought: this removes the contradiction between them, but it also removes the dialectical unity. The removal of being, then, does not in fact solve the contradiction. On the contrary, it betrays the fact that in Hegel's presentation of the problem no true unity exists. In Feuerbach's words: "One can only deduce being from thought by first tearing apart the true unity of the two, by first abstracting the soul and the essence from being and then

16

(after the event) rediscovering in this essence, abstracted from being, the sense and the principle of being emptied of itself."[5] And again: "The hegelian thesis that nature, reality, is founded on the Idea, is merely a rationalisation of the theological doctrine that nature is created by God, that material being is created by an immaterial, i.e. abstract being."

A *real* unity of thought and being, of subject and object, can only be reached by going beyond the *formal* unity of Hegel. The dialectic is the basis of Hegel's philosophy, it is his legacy; but in order to hold consistently to this dialectic, hegelian philosophy must be surmounted. Marx and Engels, and Feuerbach before them, were acting in the spirit of Hegel when they rejected his idealist thesis. Their materialist inversion of Hegel was not an arbitrary act but a demand of the dialectic. The critique of hegelian idealism is not a purely empirico-practical one — its roots are in hegelian theory itself. Hegelian philosophy already bears within itself the seed of its own destruction: it is "transcended" [*aufgehoben*] by Marx, that is to say it is negated and maintained at the same time. The dialectical unity of consciousness and being, of subject and object, must be based on the *reality* of *both* elements (in contrast to Hegel); these elements are distinct but are also in unity with each other. According to Feuerbach, "Being, from which philosophy sets out, cannot be separated from consciousness, nor consciousness from being". Being is the reality of consciousness, and consciousness the reality of being. But if being is real being, it cannot simply be the predicate of thought; it becomes, itself, subject. Feuerbach goes on to say that "the true relation of thought to being is simply this: being is subject, thought predicate. Thought proceeds from being, but being does not proceed from thought. Being exists from itself and through itself . . . being bears its principle within itself."[6]

This passage indicates the step that Feuerbach has taken from idealism to materialism. He formulates the new thesis with a precision that points forward to Marx, when he says that it is not thought which determines being but, on the contrary, social being which determines the consciousness of men.

Feuerbach does not stop there. He says critically of Hegel that his "Absolute Idea" is simply God, and his philosophy

17

simply theology. But not content with an abstract inversion of Hegel's concepts, he refuses to replace the Idea with an abstract, metaphysical version of matter — he recognises, instead, that being is *man's* being. The unity of being and thought is man; Hegel's "Idea" becomes with Feuerbach the human idea, his "self-consciousness" becomes human self-consciousness. No longer is an abstract subject confronted by a similarly abstract object. Man is the real subject. It is man who thinks; at the same time, he is also a part of objective nature. In Feuerbach's own words, "the unity of thought and being only has sense and truth if man is seen as the principle, the subject of this unity. Only a real, living being perceives real things; only where thought is not subject-for-itself but the predicate of a real living being, can we conceive of thought as inseparable from being. The unity of thought and being is therefore in no way a formal unity." The feuerbachian critique, on which Marx built, begins to surmount hegelian philosophy in the spirit of Hegel himself.

There is a further argument which proceeds from Hegel's dialectical method and rebounds on the master himself. Marx and Engels recognised the fruitful and revolutionary character of Hegel's philosophy as the fact that it dissolved the rigid definitiveness with which all previous philosophy had treated the results of human thought and action. A new concept appeared, of unending historical development: every historical stage is necessary and reasonable for a given epoch, but it is also transient and must give way to another stage, which in its turn must also pass away. In the light of this dialectical philosophy, "nothing is definitive, absolute, sacred: it reveals the transient nature of everything and in everything. Nothing can stand up before it save the uninterrupted process of becoming and passing away" (Engels: *Ludwig Feuerbach*). But Hegel sees this historical movement in idealist terms. The subject of historical movement is the Absolute Spirit. History is the process of the Spirit's self-knowledge. Men, in a mass, are the material for this movement of the Spirit. The Absolute Spirit finds adequate expression only in philosophy, which knows and perceives this movement.

The idealist dialectic reveals a double inconsistency here. First of all, the Absolute Spirit makes history only in the realm of appearance. As Marx wrote in *The Holy Family*, "the philosopher is simply the organ through which the creator of history, the Absolute Spirit, arrives at self-consciousness *in retrospect*, after the movement has ended. His participation in history is reduced to this retrospective consciousness, for the real movement is accomplished by the Absolute Spirit *unconsciously*, so that the philosopher appears *post festum*. . . . For as the Absolute Spirit only becomes conscious of itself as the creative World Spirit *post festum*, in the philosopher, so its making of history only exists in the consciousness, in the opinion and conception of the philosopher, i.e. only in speculative imagination."

This is no mere hair-splitting. Hegel fails to find a place for philosophy, the "organ of the Absolute Spirit", in the real historical process. He fails to point out that knowledge itself is a factor in history, that knowledge is not purely contemplative but has a tranformational function. He thus locates philosophy outside history, instead of seeing it as a part of history. And so, although he certainly looks at different philosophical systems in a historical light, as "the progressive development of truth" and as "moments of the organic unity", the historical development of philosophy itself remains outside real history. Hegel is therefore unable to find a solution to his own dialectical conception of history. The solution, however, springs out of it: it is the unity of theory and practice, the unity of knowledge and change.

By locating philosophical knowledge outside history, Hegel created a second inconsistency. He realised that the needs of his system had forced him to put an end to this "endless" historical process. If mankind has arrived at the point where it knows the Absolute Idea (i.e. hegelian philosophy), then this philosophy becomes Absolute Truth. Consequently, knowledge cannot develop any further: once the Absolute Spirit knows itself, the movement of history ceases. But this, of course, means that the dialectic must be eliminated. If the dialectic is to be maintained, it must therefore be taken beyond the hegelian system. The hegelian system itself turns out to have

19

been a necessary but merely temporary stage which must in its turn be surmounted.

The critique of hegeliam idealism thus had a clear direction. The real unity of thought and being could only be arrived at by re-establishing the reality of being; accordingly, history had to be seen as the real history of man. Thought was linked to being, and seen as human thought. Whereas Hegel had regarded man as the Idea's organ of self-knowledge, this "Idea" now became man's idea. Hegel had turned man into an aspect of Self-consciousness; with Marx, self-consciousness became Man's self-consciousness. The transition to the materialist thesis is made by way of the critique of hegelian philosophy, with the aid of the dialectic.

Marx thus inverted Hegel's standpoint. "With Hegel . . . the process of thinking which, under the name of 'the Idea', he even transforms into an independent subject, is the demiurge of the real world, and the real world is only the external, phenomenal form of 'the Idea' . . . With myself, on the contrary, the ideal is nothing but the material world transposed and translated in the human mind."[7] This might lead to the assumption that Marx was arguing for some kind of absolute matter, as opposed to Hegel's Absolute Idea: certainly Lenin and his followers seem to proceed from this assumption. But Marx's own doctrine was not in fact one of abstract materialism. He calls himself a "materialist", and rightly so; but in all his early writings he also stresses the fact that he is a "humanist". He makes this clear in *The Holy Family*: "Metaphysics [i.e. both the idealist and the materialist kind] will succumb forever to *materialism*, which has been perfected by the labour of speculation itself and now coincides with *humanism*." Marx did not arrive at this humanism by turning "the movement of the Idea" into metaphysical, abstract matter, but by transforming it into the real movement of human history. Marx never renounced the "humanism" of his thesis, even when later on he abandoned the term itself. This needs to be remembered, for it represents the essence of marxist theory.

In order to understand the origins of this materialist humanism correctly, we need to look again at Ludwig Feuerbach. It was he who first developed the concept, though Marx was to use it in a different sense.

The Critique of Feuerbach's Materialism

In a letter to J. B. Schweitzer (24 January 1865), Marx stated that "compared to Hegel, Feuerbach is extremely poor. All the same he was epoch-making *after* Hegel because he laid the stress on certain points . . . which were important for the progress of the critique, and which Hegel had abandoned in mystic semi-obscurity." The decisive importance of Feuerbach was that he took the step from theology to anthropology, to humanism. In his own words, "Modern philosophy is simply theology resolved into philosophy." He described Hegel's philosophy in particular as "the negation of theology from the standpoint of theology", i.e. a negation which reverted to theology. The new thesis elaborated by Feuerbach was directed against both theology and philosophical idealism simultaneously. Both, in his view, expressed the alienation of human nature. His "new philosophy", on the other hand, took man as its point of departure. "God," he wrote in the *History of the New Philosophy*, "is simply the essence of idealism, man's own spirit, which Christianity however represents as an objective being, distinct from man"; and again, in *The Essence of Christianity*, "The Absolute Being, the God of man, is his own essence." While man is seen as the essence of the Idea and of God, "the new philosophy . . . is the complete resolution of theology in anthropology. . . . The new philosophy makes man, in conjunction with nature (as the basis of man), into the unique, universal and supreme object of philosophy, and therefore makes anthropology (in conjunction with physiology) into the universal science." Feuerbach attacked idealism because it separated thought from being and turned it into an autonomous subject, whereas he himself regarded thought as the predicate of a real being, namely man.

Feuerbach thus took the decisive step from idealism to materialism and laid the foundation on which Marx and Engels were to build. The concept of "materialism", of course, had yet to be properly defined. But Marx and Engels always re-

21

garded Feuerbach as a materialist, in contrast to Max Adler and others, who saw him differently. Adler uses some of the same quotations as those above in order to prove the opposite: that Feuerbach did not proceed unilaterally from matter and always emphasised instead the unity of the ideal and the material in man. Adler labelled Feuerbach's philosophy "positivist", stating that it sought "to restrict itself to the conceptual elaboration and synthesis of given sensuous data, in order thus to arrive at the knowledge of what it calls the real."

Adler's comments (in which he links Feuerbach with Comte) are totally misplaced. Feuerbach's formulation is explicitly materialist: "Thought proceeds from being, not being from thought." Of course from time to time he poses the unity of thought and being, in fact he does so continually — but only to point out that the origin of thought is in the head of real, living man. It is an extreme dilution of his standpoint to suggest, as Adler does, that his materialism is restricted to the *material* of sense-perception as opposed to immaterial speculation. It is quite understandable that Adler, as a kantian marxist, should recoil from the apparently abstract concept of "materialism". But the fact is that neither Feuerbach nor Marx and Engels, though they consciously oppose the abstract idealism of Hegel, share this fear. On the contrary, they stress the materialism of their conception at every opportunity.

The point is, of course, that their materialism has nothing to do with abstract materialism. Adler defines "materialism" as a part of abstract metaphysics, as one of the two possible answers, supplied by metaphysics, to the question of the essence of all being: in this case, that the essence of all being is matter. If he is correct in this definition, then he is right to state that neither Feuerbach nor Marx are materialists. But in fact the materialism of both is of a different kind. Marx not only distances himself from the mechanistic materialism of natural science, as everyone knows; he also makes a clear stand against any kind of abstract, metaphysical materialism. In *The Holy Family* he refers with approval to a remark of Hegel's on the identity between idealist and materialist metaphysics:

> "On the question of Absolute Being, the Enlightenment argues with itself and is divided between two points of

view. . . . The one calls Absolute Being 'that predicateless object' . . . the other calls it matter. . . . Both are entirely the same notion."

The approving reference to this quotation, which points out the common root of metaphysical idealism and metaphysical materialism, is a clear sign that Marx rejected both kinds of metaphysics. After such a rejection, what remains of materialism? According to Adler, nothing. Adler explains Marx's use of the expression "materialist" by stating that it is intended to oppose the idealism of Hegel and his disciples, and that it is really a synonym for "anti-metaphysical". This is, of course, true as far as it goes. But if Adler thinks that the term "materialism" in Marx can simply be substituted for "realism", or "material" for "real", then he is mistaken. The accompanying counter-concept of the "ideal" would then signify "unreal", whereas Adler himself has already defined "ideal" as "that which is thought" [etwas erdachtes]. Adler, rightly, cannot accept the definition of "ideal" as "unreal", and he correctly emphasises that Marx never denied the reality of the existence of the "spiritual", of mind. But this means accordingly that "materialism", in the way Marx used the term, cannot be translated by "realism" or positivism, though undoubtedly he often used the expression "material" to mean "real". For Marx, the material is the *sensuously* real, something whose reality does not exist only in consciousness. Just as for Marx the ideal signifies consciousness, so the material is none other than being — but human being, and thus human consciousness. Marx's is a materialism where consciousness is recognised to be an aspect of the material, an aspect of being: it is "conscious being".

Feuerbach's materialism is not so clearly non-metaphysical as Marx's but even so they are in fundamental agreement on this issue. Marx calls the new theory "materialism which coincides with humanism"; Feuerbach calls it anthropology, and sometimes humanism. Materialist thought is maintained by both of them, but is rid of its abstract, metaphysical form. Being determines thought, but it is *human* being, not some kind of abstractly conceived matter. As Marx wrote in *The German Ideology*, "Consciousness can never be anything but

conscious being, and the being of man is his real life-process."
Feuerbach did not have such a clear conception. His value lies
in the fact that he saw the relationship between consciousness
and being no longer as the relation of an Absolute Idea to
being, but as the relation of human thought to the being which
forms its basis. This interpretation, which he correctly terms
"humanist", is merely Marx's starting-point. Marx continued
to be fundamentally humanist: for him, as for Feuerbach, man
stands in the middle. But it is Marx alone who first turns this
quite vague concept into something concrete, and he does
this by drawing on reality and not on philosophy. This is the
first step which Marx takes beyond Feuerbach.

Up to this point, Marx had been able to endorse the essentials
of Feuerbach's critique of Hegel. He saved himself the job of
arguing his own divergence from hegelian philosophy in systematic detail. His many references to Hegel are in fact scat-
tered and isolated. He certainly regarded the critique of religion
and theology as settled, by Feuerbach; the latter's critique of
theology was also a critique of philosophical idealism. Marx
thus found that the basis for the new materialist, humanist
doctrine had already been laid. Seen in this light, the point at
which he began to go beyond Feuerbach seemed at first to be
quite small and incidental. The point was that Marx's concept
of *man* was no longer the same as Feuerbach's. Feuerbach's
concept was abstractly philosophical: Marx drew his from real,
life, and made the concept concrete.
    This small step was, however, the decisive one. It paved the
way from speculative philosophy to a sociology based on experience. This was the step which enabled Marx to link the
theory of scientific socialism to the actual struggle of the proletariat; it led to that unity of theory and practice which distinguishes marxism from every other, purely contemplative
science. The existence of marxism dates from 1844-45, the
moment of the split from Feuerbach. One senses the feeling of
triumph in the *Critique of Hegel's "Philosophy of Law"*
(1844), in the *Theses on Feuerbach* (1845), and in *The German
Ideology* (1845-46). Marx makes his critique of Feuerbach with

the dialectic as his theoretical tool, which Feuerbach had used inconsistently.

In the sixth thesis on Feuerbach, he describes how "Feuerbach resolves the religious essence into the *human* essence. But the human essence is not abstraction inherent in each single individual. In its reality it is the ensemble of the social relations." Feuerbach regards man as a philosophical being. To the extent that man enters into reality (physiology is a part of anthropology, according to Feuerbach), he is a natural being. "The human essence" is the being of an isolated man, dominated exclusively by natural laws. When Feuerbach is forced to put him in a context, that context is simply his relationship to his fellow men as a member of the same species. In accordance with his view of man as a purely natural being, Feuerbach aptly draws the name for his new science, "anthropology", from the natural sciences.

Marx, on the other hand, never tires of defining man as a social being. "Man is no abstract essence perched somewhere outside the world. Man is the world of man, the state, society." And again: "The individual is *the social being*. His life, even if it may not appear in the direct form of a communal life carried out together with others, is therefore an expression and confirmation of *social life*." Man, Feuerbach's purely natural being, thus becomes a social being, who can only live in and through society. Purely natural laws are supplemented by social laws. Marx regards man not merely as the product of nature but as the product of social, human labour. It is not only consciousness that distinguishes men from animals but the fact that they produce their own means of existence. "They themselves indirectly produce their own life. . . . World history is simply the production of man through human labour". Social laws, therefore, overtake the natural laws on which they are founded.

Feuerbach overlooks this and is forced to abstract from the movement of history. He recognises what he calls "the religious disposition" as a human characteristic but not as a social one, for he sees it as a constant, without historical development. He is consequently unable to examine properly how religion is to be "dissolved" by his critique of it: the demands of man's unvarying "religious disposition" would contradict this. He can only propose that religion will be dissolved by enlightenment, that is to say by means of a non-material change which takes place purely at the level of consciousness. The result is that he either ignores historical change completely (as in his concept of man), or he has a purely idealist view of it. Marx was right to say that "to the extent that Feuerbach is a materialist, history does not occur for him; and to the extent that he takes history into consideration, he is no materialist".

The final point of of Marx's critique of Feuerbach is the accusation that he, like all previous materialists, saw "reality . . . only in the form of the object, or of contemplation, and not as sensuous human activity, practice, not subjectively." This purely contemplative attitude sprang from the character of pre-marxist materialism, which was linked to the natural sciences: man was confronted, fatalistically, by laws of nature which he could observe but not influence. Consequently, "the active side was [instead] developed from idealism". The idealists regarded the real movement of history only as an expression of the movement of the Idea. They realised that the transformation of thought necessarily indicated a transformation of reality also, and to this extent they developed the active side — but (as Marx points out) only in an abstract sense: "Idealism naturally does not know real, sensuous activity as such". For the idealists, therefore, activity was apparent activity, existing only in ideas. In this sense Hegel could say, "It all comes down to this point, that Truth is to be conceived and expressed not only as Substance but above all as Subject."

As in every other respect, Marx distances himself here from both tendencies. He seeks to go beyond the idealists' view of practice as apparent practice, and to link practice genuinely with theory. But at the same time he draws a sharp distinction between his own standpoint and that of the materialists (into which many of the later vulgar marxists regress, such as the social democratic supporters of the theory of a peaceful and automatic transition to socialism). Feuerbach's materialism is "natural" materialism. There is no room among men for any but purely theoretical attitudes: his critique of idealism remains a theoretical critique which does not enter the realm of the practical transformation of reality.

Marx's materialism, on the contrary, is about "revolutionary, practical-critical activity". His materialist, humanist theory enables him to make this activity for the first time into a constituent part of theory itself. He recognises that the laws which man is primarily subject to are social, i.e. human laws, and that the "circumstances" which in the past appeared to rule over man are in fact human relations, in which it is possible for man to intervene. It is therefore quite logical for Marx to conclude the *Theses on Feuerbach* with the remark that the point is no longer to interpret the world but to change it.

Our description of Marx's theory as "humanist" accords with his own description in his early writings. I have shown in detail how Marx differed both from idealism and from abstract, metaphysical materialism. While it is true that he differed from them, he also represented their synthesis. But in making the synthesis he avoided the one-sidedness of each of them and brought consciousness and being into a real unity, that of living man. In his own words, "we see here how consistent naturalism or humanism distinguishes itself both from idealism and from materialism, constituting at the same time the unifying truth of both".[8]

Marx was only able to arrive at this synthesis by removing the problem of the relation between consciousness and being from the plane of abstract speculation and assigning it to science based on experience — that is, by inserting it in reality where it belongs. Feuerbach had already taken the first step towards this, by recognising that the essence of philosophy lay in anthropology, the science of man. Feuerbach's "humanism", however, should more appropriately be termed "naturalism". He regarded man only as a species, a mere product of nature; he clung to a contemplative materialism based on the natural sciences, although his early works which so influenced Marx have little connection with the flatly mechanical, natural-science materialism of the people like Büchner, Vogt and Moleschott who followed him.

Marx, on the other hand, regards man as a social product,

and nature as human, socialised nature. There is no "unchanging nature", only nature that is changed by man, who in so doing changes his own nature too. Man does not only know nature, he also drastically reshapes it, causing outward changes on the earth's surface and even climatic changes (for example, as a result of cutting down and clearing large forests):

> "And so it happens that in Manchester, for instance, Feuerbach sees only factories and machines, where a hundred years ago only spinning-wheels and weaving-looms were to be seen, or in the Campagna of Rome he finds only pasture lands and swamps, where in the time of Augustus he would have found nothing but the vineyards and villas of Roman capitalists."[9]

Sociology is the new, all-embracing science, the science of the reality of human society. The relation between consciousness and being can now be seen from a completely different angle. Previously, man was only the subject of knowledge; now he is also its object. Marx, like Hegel, sees theory as the self-knowledge of reality. But for Hegel, this "reality" was not man but the Absolute Idea. Social man, on the other hand, knows reality as social reality, i.e. his own human reality; man is the identical subject-object of knowledge.

> "Man only avoids being lost in his object if the object becomes for him a *human* object or objective man. And this is only possible if the object becomes for him a *social* object and if he himself becomes for himself a social being, just as society becomes a being for him in this object.
>
> Therefore it is only when the objective reality becomes for man in society the reality of man's essential powers — human reality, and hence the reality of his *own* essential powers — that all *objects* become for him the *objectification of himself* . . . become *his* objects, that is, *man himself* becomes the object."[10]

This idea was previously touched on by Giambattista Vico in his remarkable *Principles of a New Science on the Nature of Peoples,* in which he explains:

> "For anyone who thinks about it, it must be a surprise to notice that all the philosophers with the utmost seriousness have made it their business to arrive at

science from the natural world (when the natural world is something which only God can have scientific knowledge of, since He created it), while they have neglected to bring their consideration to bear on the world of nations, on that civil society which men really are capable of knowing."

Marx mentions Vico occasionally, but is far enough beyond him to have eliminated the separation between the natural and the "civil" (i.e. social) world. He does this by stressing the primacy of the social, human factor, and it is this that explains the problem of the identity between humanism and naturalism which Vico touched on. Nature and man form a unity. Just as man is a product of nature (as well as the product of human labour), so too the nature which surrounds him is produced, in its present form, by human society. Once man is considered a social being, nature too is recognised as human and social. Nature is the basis for his presence in the world, the link with other men, an aspect of his social existence: "Society is the consummated oneness in substance of man and nature. . . . the naturalism of man and the humanism of nature both brought to fulfilment."[11]

Social reality knows itself: thought and being find their unity in man, who represents both subject and object. The science which deals with this is called, correctly, "humanism". The philosophical problem has become a sociological one.

CHAPTER II: The Marxian Problematic of Base and Superstructure

Base

Marx recognised the relation between being and thought as a relation between human (i.e. social) being and human consciousness. The essence of the materialist view of history is that consciousness is determined by social being. What, then, is to be understood by "social being"? Marx touched on this issue in the famous *Preface to "The Critique of Political Economy"*:

> "In the social production of their life, *people** enter into particular, necessary relations independently of their will, relations of production which correspond to a particular stage of development of their material productive forces. These productive relations as a whole form the economic structure of society, the real [*reale*] base upon which a legal and political superstructure rises and to which particular forms of social consciousness correspond. The mode of production of material life conditions the social, political and mental life process in general. It is not the consciousness of men that determines their being but, on the contrary, their social being that determines their consciousness."

The human character of being is clearly emphasised here. "The anatomy of civil society" is to be "sought in political economy". The economic structure forms the "real base" of social life. Because historical materialism gives this determining importance to "economy", it is often described as economism or as an economistic interpretation of history, comparable with all kinds of other materialist interpretations of history which are based on natural elements such as geography, race, climate etc. But this obscures the fact that historical

---

*Jakubowski's italics.

materialism already takes all these factors of nature into account. Furthermore, historical materialism is not a one-sided explanation of everything in terms of economics, in the way that the other interpretations of history explain everything in terms of race, for example, or of climate. Historical materialism does not deny the importance of natural factors, but neither does it endow them with a significance independent of economic factors: they are only important as elements of the social world, which is what human activity turns them into.

What distinguishes man from the animals is the fact that he produces the means of subsistence and labour which are necessary to him. Man's production of the means of subsistence is, from the outset, a particular expression of his mode of life. Marx wrote in *The German Ideology*, "As individuals express their life, so they are. What they are, therefore, coincides with production . . . and thus depends on the material conditions determining their production." In the first instance these conditions of production are natural conditions and can be divided into two groups: the physical constitution of man himself, and the "geological, oro-hydrographical, climatic and other natural conditions" which he encounters. The latter group, the conditions of external nature, can be subdivided from the economic point of view into natural wealth in means of subsistence (e.g. the fertility of the soil, water stocked with fish, etc.), and natural wealth in means of labour (e.g. natural waterfalls, navigable rivers, the availability of wood, metals, coal, etc.).

At the beginnings of human culture it is the first of these subdivisions which is the decisive factor, but at higher stages of development it is the second: "All historical writing must proceed from these natural foundations and from their *modification* in the course of history by the *actions of men*." Marx is referring here to a twofold process. On the one hand he points out the importance of natural factors as the foundation, premiss and condition of production. On the other hand, he demonstrates in contrast to all previous theories of materialism that it is not only natural factors that determine man but also man who increasingly determines nature. Man is not

31

simply a piece of nature, he is also a force which re-forms nature.

This leads us to a further point. Natural factors do not affect human relations directly, but only in a mediated form. A sea which separates two peoples from each other at a primitive technological stage is, at a higher stage, their means of communication. The natural geographical situation which relates England to America has not changed since prehistory, but it has taken on a wholly different meaning. The effects of natural factors therefore depend on the mediation of economic (i.e. human) relations, which have arisen on the foundation of those natural factors.

These effects are changed in the historical process. The connection between human relations and the effects of natural factors is basically a twofold one. It consists of both a decrease and an increase in the importance of natural factors to social life. Dependence on nature's given factors (such as the natural fertility of the soil, weather, climate etc.) decreases — these are factors which for the most part can be offset by "artificial" technical means; man is less dependent today on harvests, natural catastrophes etc. than he was centuries ago, and it is possible, in terms of mere technology, to avoid famine. In these respects, natural factors are less important now than they were for primitive man. But in other ways their importance increases, since man exploits nature much more than he did in former times: we need only look at the gigantic upswing in the production of coal, iron, oil and rubber to realise that man is increasingly interlocked with nature. Both the decrease and the increase in man's dependence on nature come under the heading of the "socialisation of nature". This socialisation, which we habitually refer to as the "mastery" of nature, is actually the increased interlocking of society with nature. Nature's influence over man now takes a mediated form, while it is social relationships which have direct influence.

Nature remains a "realm of necessity" on which man depends. But he is capable of regulating this dependence in a rational way, inasmuch as his knowledge of its laws improves. And he obtains this knowledge from the socialisation of nature, i.e. from his own practical transformation of nature in production.

On the foundation of these conditions of nature rise the relations of production, which in turn determine the superstructure. The relations of production, which in their totality form "the economic structure of society", should be recognised first of all as human relations. This point needs constant emphasis, for it is precisely here that the misunderstandings of Marx's theory begin to multiply. There is a widespread misconception that historical materialism can never be too materialist, a metaphysical-materialist interpretation that leads ultimately to economic fatalism. According to this interpretation economic structures and forces do as they please, independently of man. Rudolf Stammler misinterprets marxism in this way. He writes, for example, that "in the view of social materialism, social and economic phenomena are natural formations",[12] and polemicises against this view.

But when Marx and Engels speak of "natural economic laws" they are a long way from this kind of fatalism. On the contrary, they demonstrate that it is the effects of man's *own* forces which, simply as a result of the natural division of labour, confront him as alien, autonomous forces and take on the appearance of natural laws, independent of the will of individual men. This "natural" appearance of economic laws is removed when these human forces are appropriated by society, when the means of production are socialised. Men are then in a position to control the application of their own forces and are no longer at the mercy of any blind "natural economic laws". Marx and Engels emphasise this active aspect: "For the practical materialists, i.e. the communists, the point is to revolutionise the existing world, to attack and to change in practice the state of affairs they find before them."

Marx demonstrates clearly enough that it is men who have created economic relations, even if they are not fully conscious of having *precisely these* relations. Economic relations are the original unforeseeable product of an aggregation of voluntaristic impulses from individual consciousnesses; the final result does not correspond to the will of any single indivi-

33

dual. Consequently, men "enter into particular, necessary relations of production which are independent of their will." These relations emerge in historical stages which are verifiable. What these different historical stages have in common is the fact that they all regulate human co-existence in the production of the means of subsistence. The term "relations of production" cannot be used to refer to the regulation of production within a single enterprise; it refers to the economic relationships which obtain among the members of society, as a result of their participation in the process of social production.

Belonging to the relations of production there are also the relations of distribution, which according to Marx "are simply the relations of production *sub alia specie*". They are also legal relations, the relations of master and slave. In law, they appear as the relations of property, which express the cleavage of society into classes and the suppression of one part of it by another. Marx gives special emphasis to the historical and changing character of the relations of production, and distinguishes the following stages: primitive communism, the asiatic, classical, feudal and capitalist modes of production, and socialism.

The relations of production correspond to a particular level of productive forces, on whose development they depend. Here again, it is easy to misconstrue historical materialism as a natural science, for productive forces are mostly natural forces. The most important of them are the human labour force and natural energy, such as soil fertility, the heat of the sun, etc. The dependence of the relations of production on the level of productive forces might seem to demonstrate that social reality is determined unilaterally by natural factors. This is obviously what Plekhanov believes, when he traces all social relations back through the mediation of productive forces to natural geographical conditions, as "the last instance".

In reality this is not the case. Natural forces only become productive forces because they are harnessed by human labour. They only become social forces by being incorporated into human relations and applied to human ends. Natural forces, therefore, only become productive when they serve the production and reproduction of human life.

The most important productive force is human labour. It is distinct from all purely natural forces because it is applied consciously. Human production is distinct from that of even the most amazingly practical animals (such as bees and ants) by virtue of the fact that men visualise the result before they begin to produce. This makes human labour a social force, not merely a natural one. The same is true for the other productive forces, apart from labour. The conscious use of natural fertility, fire or electricity, turns them into social forces; man takes command of the often destructive effects which they have as natural forces. Outside their relationship with man they remain natural forces; but within that relationship, they assist the specifically human productive force, i.e. labour.

The development of the relations of production accentuates the social character of productive forces. The exploitation of purely natural forces is now supplemented by conditions of production which are exclusively social, such as the organisation of labour (assembly-line production, etc.). Marx wrote in *The German Ideology*: "It follows that a certain mode of production or industrial stage is always combined with a certain mode of co-operation or social stage, and this mode of co-operation is itself a productive force."

The stage of development of productive forces conditions the corresponding relations of production. Labour with machines, steam, electricity, etc. calls for the organisation of the factory; labour is divided rationally down to the last detail. This labour cannot be carried out by feudal peasants; it presupposes the existence of wage workers, some of them highly skilled. The elements of capitalism (the machine, and the increasing division of labour in manufacture and then within the factory) develop within feudalism. At a particular stage of development they begin to thrust against the limits of the old mode of production. The new, market form of capitalist production, which has pushed aside the dominant feudalist mode (based on the production of basic needs), demands unrestricted freedom of trade and business and the removal of the old restrictions and privileges. The emancipation of the peasants becomes an economic necessity, designed to establish a large national market for the commercialisation of industrial investment. The contradiction between the productive forces and the outlived mode of production manifests itself in revolutionary forms, in the social and political struggle of the economically progressive class (in the rise of capitalism, this is the bourgeoisie) against the classes which dominate under the old relations of production. In his *Contribution to the Critique of Political Economy*, Marx sums up this process as follows:

> "At a certain stage of their development, the material forces of production enter into contradiction with the existing relations of production . . . within which they have previously moved. These relations have changed, from being forms of the development of productive forces, into their chains. A period of social revolution then begins."

The development of productive forces is not conditioned solely by the forces of nature. It is also dependent on the growth in population, which creates the need for higher production and improved technical capacity. Technological progress, increased knowledge of nature and improvements in the organisation of manufacture: all this raises productivity. The most important aspect of this process is the division of labour.

The division of labour is first of all a natural division, a result of the differences in man's natural aptitudes according to age, sex, physical strength, etc. It manifests itself at first in the division of labour in the family and the division of society into separate families. The decisive step comes with the division between mental and manual labour. It now becomes "possible, indeed it is the case, that intellectual and physical activity, pleasure and labour, production and consumption, fall to the share of different individuals". At this point individuals begin to be exclusively engaged in a particular type of activity. This is bound up with the separation of society into classes; the division of labour is also an extremely unequal deployment of labour and of its means of production, and the results are property and the subjugation of the propertyless to the property owners. The ensuing contradiction between individual and general interests gives rise to the state, which is both the necessary expression of the common interest and a means of maintaining the *status quo* through the repression of the dispossessed classes.

The natural division of labour, which is not consciously controlled by man but develops organically "by itself", has the effect of making consciousness and being appear as two spheres which are independent of each other:

> "The production of ideas, of concepts, of consciousness, is at first directly interlinked with the material activity and material intercourse of men, the language of real life. . . . Men are the producers of their ideas . . . but this changes with the separation between intellectual and physical labour: from this point on, consciousness can imagine itself to be something other than consciousness of existing practice, to have become 'pure' theory."[13]

Hence the apparent autonomy of thought, the apparent separation of base from superstructure.

Superstructure

"Superstructure" in the writings of Marx and Engels is a very broad and indeterminate concept. It embraces the whole of social life apart from its "real base", the direct relations of production. The economy is assigned a special place in the totality of social relations, the foundation of which is the production of immediate subsistence. This does not mean that economic relations are to be strictly separated from the rest, nor that they can be, even in a purely conceptual sense. The unity of social life is so strong that the only possible distinction is a methodological one, for the purpose of throwing light on any particular one of the fundamental relationships. It is a complete mistake to think that Marx's differentiation between base and superstructure was an absolute distinction between two different, unoverlapping spheres. All we can do is make a very general *paraphrase* of the concept of "superstructure". It cannot be determined *concretely*, and it certainly does not mean that a comprehensive tabulation of all social relationships is possible.

However, it is possible to distinguish the contrasting pair "base and superstructure" from other such pairs. For example, base and superstructure should not be identified with that other contrasting pair, being and consciousness. Social being is certainly founded in the economy, but it is not restricted to it; social relationships, though essentially they are determined economically, reappear in the various concrete forms of the superstructure, for example in legal, political or religious relations. Similarly, superstructure cannot be identified with consciousness; it does not consist solely of ideas but embraces some highly "material" relations — political ones, for example. Any analysis of the extent to which ideological and material relationships interpenetrate must be made individually, according to each particular case; such an analysis will reveal that all the above-mentioned concepts interpenetrate *dialectically*. But in order to arrive at this point, one first has to make a clear methodological distinction between those concepts.

Marx and Engels made some important comments on this question which may serve as our point of departure. In his *Preface to "The Critique of Political Economy"* Marx wrote of the economic structure of society as the "real base upon which legal and political superstructure rises and to which particular forms of social consciousness correspond". It might seem from this as if Marx regarded only legal and political relations as belonging to the superstructure, and not social ideas. On the other hand, in *The Eighteenth Brumaire of Louis Bonaparte* he wrote:

> "Upon the different forms of property, upon the social conditions of existence, rises an entire superstructure of distinct and peculiarly formed sentiments, illusions, modes of thought and views of life. The whole class creates and forms them out of its material foundations and out of the corresponding social relations. The single individual, who receives them through tradition and upbringing, may imagine that they form the real motives and the starting point for his own activity."

Here Marx seems to be saying the opposite, that only ideas etc. belong to the superstructure. The apparent contradiction is resolved in the following passage from Engels's letter to J. Bloch (21 September 1890):

> "The economic situation is the base, but the various elements of the superstructure — political forms of the

class struggle and its consequences . . . forms of law and then even the reflections of all these actual struggles in the brains of the combatants: political, legal and philosophical theories, religious ideas — also wield their influence upon the course of historical struggles and in many cases are the main contributors to determining the forms of these struggles."

He distinguishes here two forms of superstructure, though in reality they cannot be strictly separated, as I shall show later. The two forms correspond to each of the two meanings of "superstructure" given by Marx. I shall therefore make a distinction between political and legal superstructure on the one hand, and social ideas (which for the sake of clarity I shall call "ideological superstructure") on the other. It needs to be stressed that this kind of division, which is getting close to the model worked out by Plekhanov, is only a crude approximation to Marx's concept. The point is that a "crude" but concrete exposition of it is the necessary but merely preliminary step in combating the crude, schematic finality of theories such as Plekhanov's. The interaction of several mechanically separated planes (even if he does define a single origin for all of them) has nothing to do with the dialectic. Plekhanov distinguishes the following stages:

1. The "state of productive forces".
2. The economic relations which they determine.
3. The social and political order which rises on this economic "base".
4. The social psychology of man, which is determined in part directly by the economy, and in part by the social and political order.
5. Various ideologies which reflect the characteristics of this psychology.

By "social psychology" Plekhanov evidently means the general reaction of men, at the level of consciousness, to the social relations under which they live in a given epoch. However, this reaction manifests itself in the various concrete ideologies and is inseparable from them. Therefore by leaving out the fourth stage and condensing the first two, we are left with the following model:

1. The economic base, conditioned by productive forces.
2. The legal and political order.
3. The ideological superstructure, which "crowns" the model.

This distinction, though crude, is a methodologically necessary step in the approximation to reality. But in order to get closer still to reality, the individual elements must be presented in their correlative context and the initial conceptual distinction transcended. The point here is not so much to demonstrate that the individual spheres of the superstructure *are* correlative; few would dispute that the individual spheres influence each other, and there is a multitude of cases where this can be verified convincingly. The point is that marxism differs from all other theories of sociology by regarding the various spheres as *moments of a whole*. That "whole" is social life, which is founded on the production of material life and whose individual spheres, on this same foundation, interact not only with each other but also with the base. (In this particular sense there might seem to be some justification for saying that historical materialism is a monist theory, a kind of economism; but this is too narrow a definition, bringing out only one of its essential features.)

Let us make a closer analysis of the relationship of the superstructural forms (political, legal and ideological) to their base.

The political and legal superstructure has particularly close links to the base. According to Engels, economically determined social relationships find their expression in political and legal forms. This is not, of course, to say that every political relationship directly represents an economic one. Usually a whole series of connecting links intervenes between political and economic relations, so that there is no directly visible connection between the two. Political events have a seeming autonomy and independence which conceal the fact that political relations are the expression (more or less adequate for the purpose) of particular economic factors. Every economic era creates the kind of state which corresponds to its needs, but with every such state there is a tendency, from the beginning, towards autonomy. An imprecise analysis will therefore always tend to make the state and the economy seem like two independent factors with different origins, which meet only when they react on each other.

The emergence of the state presupposes a relatively highly developed division of labour. On the one hand, it presupposes that human labour is already productive enough to ensure that not all physically capable individuals actually carry out directly productive labour for their own means of subsistence, but they are already in a position to be employed on social interests which do not directly coincide with their own interests as individuals. On the other hand, the emergence of the state presupposes that there is already an opposition between individual and social interests; that production and appropriation no longer occur socially, as in primitive communism, but that appropriation takes place by means of exchanges among individuals. This mode of production causes society to split into classes, which are distinguished from each other by their position in the production process; the main result of this is that conflict occurs between those classes which possess the means of production and those which do not. This is why the state becomes necessary.

> "It is the admission that this society has got itself entangled in insoluble contradiction and is cleft into irreconcilable antagonisms which it is powerless to exorcise. But in order that these antagonisms, classes with conflicting economic interests, shall not consume themselves and society in fruitless struggle, a power, apparently standing above society, has become necessary to moderate the conflict and keep it within the bounds of 'order'; and this power, arisen out of society but placing itself above it and increasingly alienating itself from it, is the state."[14]

This state, which arises from the conflict between classes, is "as a rule, the state of the most powerful, economically dominant class, which by this means also becomes the politically dominant class and thus acquires new means of holding down and exploiting the oppressed class". For every stage of the relations of production there is a particular, corresponding

41

form of state, which regulates the relations between the different classes to the advantage of the economically dominant class:

> "The ancient state was, above all, the state of the slave-owners for holding down the slave, just as the feudal state was the organ of the nobility for holding down the peasant serfs and bondsmen, and the modern representative state is the instrument for exploiting wage-labour by capital."[15]

This state, however, has an inherent tendency towards autonomy, a tendency to alienate itself from the society from which it was born. With the increase in the division of labour the state grows in importance as the organiser of social life. Its accumulating functions are no longer limited simply to representing the ruling class against the oppressed class and against the classes of other countries: it begins to concern itself with the economic and cultural interests of the society as a whole, though naturally this is a process which continues to be to the advantage of the ruling class. As the state grows more important, the state apparatus and the autonomy of movement of this apparatus also grow, and this has fundamental repercussions, both good and bad, on the economic base. At this point the state has to insert its own needs (taxes, tariffs etc.) directly into economic life, and in the process of doing this it can sometimes harm the interests of the ruling class which it is trying to serve.

The state acquires a particularly high degree of autonomy where there is an even balance of forces between the classes. The absolute monarchies of the seventeenth and eighteenth centuries were strong because the power of the nobility and the bourgeoisie was evenly balanced, though even in this case the state cannot be said to have been independent of the relations of production. Absolutism was still based partly on feudal forces, whose political rights it upheld (even if in a somewhat reduced form) and whose economic existence it guaranteed by maintaining serfdom. On the other hand it had already begun to build on the growing bourgeoisie, representing the latter's economic interests by introducing the mercantilist policies which were needed for the development of modern industry. As soon as the bourgeoisie had established clear economic superiority this state was destroyed and gave way to another, which could express the bourgeoisie's economic domination in a political form. The bonapartism of the first and especially the second French empires, where bourgeoisie and proletariat had fought each other to a standstill, is another example of the relative autonomy of the state apparatus. Modern fascism, too, comes partly under this heading: an even balance of forces between capital and labour puts the petty bourgeois layers in political control, although they do not have any influence on the economic foundations of capitalism and are obliged to carry out policies in favour of the bourgeoisie, which is still the economically dominant class.

The state, therefore, only *seems* to be autonomous in relation to the economic base. It is still economically determined, in spite of the periods when there is an apparently growing tendency towards autonomy. It is true, however, that the increasing division and specialisation of labour forces the state to take over more and more economic functions. The correlation between state and economy becomes more explicit at this point, and reaches a peak when the state is actually controlled by the proletariat, in the dictatorship of the proletariat. Here, state and economy directly coincide. The proletarian state is the expression of the proletariat's economic dominance. The tendency then is for the state, with the socialisation of the means of production and the disappearance of classes, to wither away (since it was originally the product of class antagonisms). In the USSR, which in spite of the extent of bureaucratisation can still be referred to as an example of a proletarian state, the economy is above all a state economy, and the state an economic state.

The statement that for every economic era there is a particular, corresponding form of state, must not be looked at as a mere formula but must be examined in concrete ways. It is certainly true to say that capitalism has its own corresponding form of state which expresses the political domination of the bourgeoisie; but it need not necessarily follow that one and the same form of state prevails in all capitalist countries. (Social democratic theoreticians, for example, tend to make a rigid formula of the "democratic republic", which they regard as the necessary preliminary to socialism and the rule of the proletariat.) One of the basic principles of the dialectic is the law of uneven development. This unevenness is obvious from the diversity of forms which capitalism has taken in different countries. The diversity cannot be accounted for only by the differences in natural factors (climate, race, geography etc.) which the expanding capitalist market encounters; there is also a whole series of socio-historical factors which comes into play. The forms of state are as diverse as the forms of capitalist economy to which they correspond. They have only one essential feature in common, which is that they express the domination of the bourgeoisie.

The unevenness of economic development is particularly evident in the phenomenon known as "combined development". In most countries capitalism does not develop in a simple, organic way out of the decay of feudal forms, but as a result of importing more modern forms of organisation of production from other, more highly-developed countries. In the colonial areas it is usual for capitalism to intervene in precisely this way, and to undermine the older economic forms. The result here is that many kinds of feudal and semi-feudal relations, especially in agriculture, co-exist with large and technically advanced capitalist concerns. This phenomenon has played an extremely important role in large parts of Europe (prewar Russia, the Balkans, Eastern Europe) and even more so outside Europe, and has produced a diversity of concrete forms of capitalism, with a whole series of political consequences. In its struggle against feudalism the rising bourgeoisie is the bearer of broadly liberal ideas which express the struggle for economic freedom and the breaking of the old feudal barriers (this can be observed in various forms from the pre-revolutionary bourgeoisies in France and England to the Chinese bourgeoisie of the present day).

The other feature of combined development is that a relatively strong proletariat springs up at the same time as the bourgeoisie. Concentrated in the large firms and influenced by the theory and practice of the foreign workers' movement, this proletariat develops a strong class consciousness even before the emancipation of the bourgeoisie, and plays its own independent revolutionary role. The workers in the great French revolution developed no autonomous ideology but simply formed the left wing of the bourgeoisie, since the latter put the ideas of liberalism into practice with consistency and revolutionary *élan*. But by 1848, the behaviour of the German bourgeoisie, for example, was already quite different. Dithering between opposition to absolutism on the one hand and fear of the growing proletariat on the other, it led a feeble struggle from the very outset. By 1917 this process was clearer still. The Russian liberal bourgeoise's fear of the proletariat prevented it from being able to carry out its own bourgeois revolution with any thoroughness at all.

Combined development of the economy thus produces its own specific political forms. Where the bourgeoisie is incapable of carrying out a thorough-going bourgeois revolution, the proletariat appears at the forefront. It not only carries out those measures which are specific to the bourgeois revolution (e.g. political democracy, the distribution of land), it also links these with socialist measures. The ensuing form of state has tendencies towards the dictatorship of the proletariat and symptoms of socialist revolution; it appeared in all the post-war revolutions (Russia 1917, Germany and Austria 1918, China 1926, Spain 1931, etc.). It is clearly distinct from the "old" bourgeois democratic state, and expresses the proletariat's position as the leading class in the revolutionary process. As long as this superiority remains, the tendency towards "permanent revolution" and the dictatorship of the proletariat remains. But in these circumstances it is possible for the bourgeoisie to recover, to liquidate the state created by the revolution and erect its own, stronger form of direct dictatorship. Examples of this are the Austrian dictatorship after 1934, the attempt at a bourgeois dictatorship in Germany between 1930 and 1932, and the dictatorship of the formerly revolutionary Kuomintang in China. Another "combined" form of political domination is current in Japan, where it takes the form of joint rule by the feudal nobility and the capitalists, a result of the grafting of capitalist industries on to semi-feudal forms of agriculture.

These few sketchy examples show how particular capitalist economic relations in various countries are expressed through corresponding forms of state. There are also many cases where political factors can be seen to be explicit forms of economic struggle. Different political parties express the economically determined needs of different social layers. Conversely, economic organisations such as trade unions and employers' unions often fight battles which not only have political effects but must be described as actual political struggles.

The legal superstructure stands even closer than the political superstructure to the economic base. The state is only rarely a *direct* expression of economic relationships; more often, the political superstructure consists of a sum of relationships which correspond to this base but have developed a certain autonomy of their own. Law is different. Economic relationships often make their appearance directly in legal form. Marx spoke of "the relations of production or, what is only a legal expression for this . . . the relations of property". He identifies the two concepts with each other. He explains this identification in a passage in *Capital,* where he says that the precondition of commodity exchange is the commodity owners' recognition of each other in law as proprietors who unite in the process of that exchange:

> "This legal relation, which takes the form of a contract, whether such contract be part of a developed legal system or not, is a relation between two wills, which reflects the economic relation. The content of this relation is given by the economic relation itself."[16]

The legal relation thus expresses an economic relation simply by being the form of that relation. It is hardly necessary to add that the judicial forms of private or civil law which are centred on the concept of property, express economic factors, or that sale and purchase, rent, mortgage, indentured labour, are legal concepts which directly express particular economic relationships.

The appearance of economic relations in legal form is a general feature of capitalism. However, this legal form does not necessarily express the social and economic content of the relation as it really is. A labour contract, for example, appears to be an agreement between two equals, the employer and the worker; but in reality, this contract is simply the form assumed by the social inequality between the two partners and by the economic exploitation of the proletarian. The legal relation "reflects" social reality in a distorted, reified form. It has the appearance of equality in what is actually inequality — the exchange of different, unequal kinds of commodity (labour power and money), the dependent position of the proletarian who has only his labour power to sell, etc. — and the appearance of an "exchange of things" masking what is actually a form of human domination. This whole reified appearance is itself a crucial element of capitalism. Law is an important form of capitalist ideology.

I have shown that the economic relation is the *content* of the legal relation, but what of the legal *form* itself? Law is essentially form. Kelsen, the most coherent spokesman of the kantian school, regards laws as form alone. Its sole meaning for him is the formal, logical deducibility of norms of various grades from each other. He sees law as a complex of such norms at the level of "ought" [*das Sollen*], which is strictly separate from the level of "being". Since legislation is obviously an aspect of being, it cannot belong with law, which is an aspect of "ought"; therefore legislation, individual laws and their practical efficacy are topics for investigation by sociology, not law. This allows him to claim that the *content* of law is supplied by social relations but that its *form* remains completely independent, a norm of "ought" determined by another "ought" and not by social and economic being.

The kantian dualism between "ought" and being may allow the form of law to be separated from its content, but the dialectical approach of marxism certainly does not. "Form has no validity except as the form of its content," wrote Marx. Form and content make up an inseparable unity. Consequently, there must be a connection between legal form and economic relations. The analysis of the commodity form provides the key to this problem.

In capitalism, production is social but appropriation is private; the producer and the consumer are not identical. It is

47

true that production takes place for social needs; but it is not regulated socially. Individual capitalists produce what they want and exchange their products for others. In this kind of social order the various products must be reduced, regardless of their *qualitative* diversity, to a uniform *quantitative* measure so that they can be compared and exchanged. The products of human labour thus take on the character of commodities, which confront each other in value form as quantitatively comparable. The various forms of concrete labour are transformed into abstract labour, which constitutes the uniform basis of all the various kinds of commodity and makes them measurable.

"Since commodities do not exchange themselves", their owners have to meet each other for the purposes of exchange. Commodity owners are not just any random set of individuals, exchanging commodities as they please. Since in the capitalist social order commodities rule men rather than the other way round, and since economy determines life, commodity owners are the mere *representatives* of their commodities, and the act of exchange is forced on them. "The characters who appear on the economic stage", the commodity owners, "are simply the personification of the economic relations that exist between them." In order to be able to exchange their goods as commodities, the commodity owners must "place themselves in relation to one another as persons whose will resides in those objects which they exchange. . . . They must therefore recognise each other as private proprietors". The commodity owners meet as legal subjects with equal rights.

The general value form of commodities, which makes it possible to compare them, has a corresponding general legal form: that of legal subjectivity, which recognises all men as formally equal, as having the same legal capacity. Man the commodity owner is a legal subject, of equal rank to every other legal subject, and has the legal capacity to exchange whatever commodities he possesses. There is no difference here between the commodity "means of production or consumption" and the commodity "labour power". In a formal sense, both these commodities have the same value, a value determined by the labour time which is socially necessary to manufacture them. Thus

48

the generality of legal form and of the underlying concept of legal subjectivity correspond to the generality of the commodity form in capitalism. Formerly, economic domination appeared as such and the corresponding legal forms were also seen to be what they were: relations of dependence and inequality (as in serfdom). The legal form and the commodity form work their way into the existing relations hand in hand. As a relatively independent political power develops, serving the interests of the ruling class as a whole, so too does public law. Public law regulates the relations between the state and public institutions, and between these and the citizens; it serves to execute and protect private or civil law by means of the power of the state. The foundation for all these relations is still legal subjectivity and the recognition of the legal capacity of man, which give the relations of domination a general form.

Once law has emerged, it develops a relative autonomy. It preserves old legal forms, supplying them with new content, and creates new forms whose connection with the economic base can only be traced through a series of mediations. Legal capacity, for example, is separate from commercial capacity; it is no longer bestowed only on men but also on "legal entities". The connection with the economic base becomes less and less visible. In a letter to Conrad Schmidt (27 October 1890), Engels wrote:

> "In a modern state, law must not only correspond to the general economic situation and be its expression, but it must also be an expression which is in itself consistent, and which does not, owing to inner contradictions, rebound against itself. And in order to achieve this, the faithful reflection of economic relations is thereby more and more interfered with."

Even from this brief account, we can see that the correlation between the legal and political superstructure and its economic base is not superficial, that the two elements form a unity. Up to this point our discussion has been restricted to the determination of the superstructure by the base. Before we can look at the interactions which take place within the unity between the two, it is necessary to demonstrate how

49

the ideological superstructure relates to the legal and political superstructure and to the base.

We have already seen how the political and legal superstructure is distinct from the ideological superstructure. The former represent the form in which class struggles occur; the latter is the form in which men become conscious of these struggles. This does not mean that the two spheres are autonomous or separate from each other, and connected externally if at all. The separation is a methodological one only: in reality, they form moments of a unity. The ideas of men are a constituent part of political and legal relations: ideas in the sense of ideology as a whole, not simply political and legal ideas. The individual spheres of human thought form a totality, which is the intellectual structure of society, as opposed to the material structure. But this "as opposed to" does not imply a fundamental differentiation between the two. Consciousness is conscious being, a constituent part of being. We can only understand the interaction among the various elements correctly if we first recognise their unity. I shall therefore attempt to ascertain this correlative unity between legal and political relations and the ideas which correspond to them.

According to the prevailing kantian theory of law, law is a complex of norms, a sum of imperatives. Kelsen, the most coherent of the kantian juridical theoreticians, constantly stresses the fact that law is exclusively a normative science which exists only at the level of "ought". The facticity of law consists in this normativity; the being of law is the being of "ought". In other words, law exists only in the sphere of the idea.

But looked at from a non-kantian, dialectical standpoint, law does have a material existence. The reality of law is not merely the reality of human ideas: legal ideas are only the expression of material relations reflected in the forms of law. Even Kelsen cannot ignore this reality completely. At the point where he is obliged to assign a theoretical significance to the *application* of law, he concedes that there is necessarily a certain amount of tension between the "legality" of a norm and its application if the norm itself is to have any value. That is to

50

say, if legal norms are not actually applied they remain a dead letter. Law, therefore, exists in fact, as the form of particular material relations. With the universality of the commodity form under capitalism, law exists as the general form of the capitalist relations of production; it is at the same time the abstract expression of these material relations, their legal norm. But law also exists as material reality, in the sense of legal practice, contracts, trials, acts of administration etc., and of individual laws. The two forms are linked in modern law. Logically, individual legal relations are *deduced* from general norms and represent their *concretisation*. Historically, it is the other way round: it is the particular development of the practice of legal life that *produces* general norms, which represent the *abstraction* of those individual legal relations (the development of primitive casuistic legal norms into the highly abstract laws of today clearly indicates such a process). This close interconnection between the general and particular forms of law is an aspect of its permanent development: on the one hand abstract norms originate from practical usage, and on the other hand it becomes necessary to present these abstract norms as the logical basis of concrete legal relations. "That form of law which is expressed in logical abstractions is a product of real or concrete legal form . . . , of the real mediation of the relations of production."[17]

Human ideas form an essential part of the political superstructure, just as they do of the legal superstructure. Although the state's specific purpose is to suppress the economically dominated classes, i.e. although it is a coercive state, it rarely does the job by pure force. Usually the oppressed classes freely obey; consciousness of the fact that the state is willing and able to achieve its aims by force, if necessary, is sufficient. This "idea" is an essential constituent of political life. It is only because of this that political life proceeds with a certain calm, a relative lack of friction.

This general conception of the power of the state is not the only idea which forms part of the state's existence; there is also the consciousness that this power is necessary. The dominated classes, the majority of society, are not conscious of it as a historical necessity but as a permanent one, which prevents ongoing opposition. The lack of a developed proletarian class consciousness is thus vital to the existence of the capitalist state. If the state apparatus is to maintain the class rule of the bourgeoisie in a period when the objective economic conditions for its defeat are already a reality, then to have a monopoly on the ownership of weapons is not enough. The maintenance of bourgeois rule requires also that the proletariat and the other oppressed layers have no clear socialist consciousness. If the proletariat had this consciousness it would not only be able to see the class struggle, it would also be able to recognise capitalism as a merely historical stage of development, situated at a particular level of productive forces. This in turn would open the way to the possibility of a dictatorship of the proletariat, whose task would be to create the preconditions for a classless society and lead the transition towards it. Bourgeois democracy is only possible as long as it prevents the development of these ideas: it is therefore a form of state in which the oppressed classes participate in the maintenance of bourgeois rule.

Every form of state creates its corresponding ideologies, which are an essential part of its existence. One of the ideas which a democracy needs if it is to function properly is the idea that democracy is the most suitable form of state. Once the state's belief in its own suitability weakens, then, whatever the material foundation for this weakening may be, it becomes unable to function. In a monarchy, the idea of legitimacy (and in an absolute monarchy, the idea of divine right) plays a similar role. A dictatorship cannot exist forever if the great majority of the people is convinced that the dictator is incapable of leading.

Finally, the ideological conceptions of politically active individuals and groups not only supply the subjective *motivation* for actions which are rooted objectively in economic and social being, they also *determine* this activity and the particular forms it takes.

Political and legal superstructure have necessarily been dealt with at some length, since their position between the economic base and ideological superstructure brings out the links between the two. One of those links, which we have dealt with already, is the complex of political and legal ideas which belong to the ideological superstructure; their connection with the base is, as we have seen, mediated by political and legal relations of a "material" kind. This mediation occurs to a varying degree in all the spheres of the ideological superstructure.

But before analysing the relationship of human ideas and ideological superstructure to the economic base, we must first of all understand that not every individual sphere of the ideological superstructure has its own particular corresponding sphere in material being. Economic, political and legal ideas correspond to economic, political and legal relations. But the same cannot be said for scientific or religious ideas. What can be said, however, is that all these various spheres of ideas correspond *in their totality*, as the intellectual structure of society, to its economic structure. In their own specific ways they express the whole of the respective society; that is to say, in the concrete form of their subject-matter and the way in which they are viewed and presented, they express the relations of production.

The dependence of ideological superstructure on its material base in generally indirect. Just as in the case of political and legal superstructure, every sphere of ideas tends to develop in its own way once it has been cut off from its roots by the division between manual and mental labour. "Economy creates nothing directly, *a novo*, but it determines the way in which the existing material of thought is transformed and developed" (Engels). This effect occurs indirectly, though the mediation of political, legal and moral "reflections" of the economy. The connection is thus not an obvious one, and only a detailed analysis of individual cases can unearth it.

It is relatively easy to prove the connection in cases where the division of labour is not so highly developed: for example, the connection between a primitive religion or philosophy of nature and the economic relations of a tribe, or the origins of musical form in rhythms of work. In a society with a highly developed division of labour, the connection is most clearly visible in the process of great revolutionary upheavals. In these cases it is obvious that social relations are in constant change

53

and development, that they are not a permanent condition. The reciprocal influence of base and superstructure and their interaction within the unity of social life, can only be verified during the process of a revolution in these relations — a constant process which proceeds dialectically, i.e. continuously *and* in leaps.

The great French revolution, for example, was the political expression of a displacement of economic and social power in favour of the bourgeoisie. This displacement found its philosophical expression in rationalism and the materialism of the Encyclopaedists. None of these theoreticians was conscious of the connection between their work and the emancipation of the third estate. Even where philosophical theories were linked to political ones, as they sometimes are in Rousseau, it was never the interests of the bourgeoisie which were invoked but those of "man" or "society". Some historians have noted, with the advantage of hindsight, that these theories contributed to the preparation of the revolution. But all they are actually saying (and this none too clearly) is that like the political revolution itself, these theories were the product of the contemporary social antagonisms, that they expressed and "solved" those antagonisms in their own ideological way while the political revolution solved them in a practical way.

Thomas Münzer is another example. He led the economically generated social struggle of the peasantry and urban plebs against the feudal princes and barons. The struggle itself took a political form, but his consciousness of the struggle took a religious form. Acting for the people against the barons, he spoke of "pushing the ungodly from the seat of judgement and raising the rude and lowly". Social oppression appeared to him as religious sin, and he called himself "God's knight battling against the ungodly". It is not difficult to recognise the connection between the two spheres in this example; but in other cases it can only be proved by a careful analysis of all the interconnecting links between them.

There is one stage in the superstructure which we have not so far dealt with, and that is what Plekhanov inserted between political and ideological superstructure: the "psychology of social man". It would be a mistake to think of this as anything like a "psychic structure" of society, as if it were a separate stage of the superstructure. Engels, in a letter to Mehring (14 November 1893), wrote:

"We all laid and were bound to lay the main emphasis at first on the derivation of political, legal and other ideological notions from basic economic facts. But in so doing we neglected the formal side — the way in which these notions come about."

This question has been similarly neglected in marxist literature ever since. It is a task which only an analytic social psychology can carry out. Ideologies do not emerge directly from the relations of production: they are produced by men. They are the products of particular desires, impulses, interests and needs, which for their part are biologically determined and then quantitatively and qualitatively structured by the socio-economic situation. Ideologies are their rationalisation. Psychology thus has two problems to deal with. One is to explore the instinctual apparatus which, in the particular form it achieves by being transformed in the social process, belongs to the "base", defined in this context as the very constitution of man, his own "nature". The other problem is to demonstrate how "the economic situation is transposed into ideology via instinctual life". The investigation of these questions makes it easier to apply historical materialism to particular, concrete sets of relations.

But historical materialism itself is not a theory of motivation. It is based on the thesis that social life is determined by economic *relations*; it must not be confused with a science that regards economic *interests* as the only historically effective motive. Marx is often misrepresented in this way, as in Hendrik de Man's book, *Towards a Psychology of Socialism*, for example. In it, he tries to refute Marx by foisting ideas on him which he did not hold: "Every economic theorem and every strategic political opinion of Marx rests on the presupposition that the motivation of human will, through which social progress occurs, is based first of all on economic interests." Marxism in no way denies the existence of non-economic motives. Although the term "economic causes" may be used, "economy" is not seen as a subjective, psychological motivation but as the objective condition of human life. In

55

Engels's words, "there is no inconsistency in the fact that *ideal* driving forces are recognised; the inconsistency comes about when the investigation is not carried beyond these and back into their motive causes", which lie in the economic and social situation.

Let us examine another attempt to determine the content of the superstructure, that of Carl Brinkmann. We find that he distinguishes three layers: law and custom, science and technology, art and religion. Apart from the fact that this is not an exhaustive list (for example, the state is not included), it suffers from another vital flaw. The concepts are viewed in a quite undialectical way as static, though in actual fact it is only their functional, non-static form that gives them any meaning. They cannot be treated as autonomous layers independent of each other, but only as correlating and interacting spheres. The problem of whether to assign this or that relationship to the economic base or to the superstructure depends entirely on its concrete function. In Brinkmann's static conception, science and technology would certainly belong to the superstructure. But as Marx pointed out, the natural sciences are a productive force, and this means that they can be assigned to the base. The same is true of technology and also, to some extent, of management science (science-based rationalisation as a factor in production). Only a functional conceptual structure can prevent the rigidification of categories and afford an adequate knowledge of reality.

The base and the various stages of superstructure are only separable methodologically. It is evident that they are constituent parts of an indivisible whole, which is the process of social life; these parts are constantly changing and affecting each other. (The significance of this methodological distinction will be dealt with in the next section.)

In order to combat a widespread misunderstanding, it must be stressed that the superstructure is real. Lenin in particular tended to overlook this, when he contrasted being and idea in his "reflection theory". The superstructure is no less real than its base. The terms "reflection" and "to reflect", which Engels was fond of using when he was discussing ideological superstructure, can be misleading; these terms are meant to

56

indicate something about the *relationship* between base and superstructure, not to *describe* the superstructure itself. There are in fact two forms of reality: the material reality and the "ideal" reality (i.e. the reality of human ideas). Political and legal superstructure are as real as the base. Both are social relations consisting of human relationships. Both exist in the idea, both are also material realities. As Marx said in *The Holy Family*, "The communist workers know full well that property, capital, money, wage labour etc. are in no way the mere creations of their imagination but are the extremely concrete and practical results of their own self-alienation", and the same is true of non-economic relationships. The reality of social ideas, then, forms a necessary and constituent part of the material reality of social relationships. *Material relations are what they are only in conjunction with the ideas which correspond to them.* The reality of both is expressed by their social efficacy.

When Marx made the leap from natural to human, social being, he enabled us to recognise the unity between social life and the ideas which form a part of that life. There is no social being without consciousness and, conversely, consciousness is nothing but conscious being.

The main weight of our argument so far has gone into demonstrating that the superstructure depends on its economic foundations. But it is necessary to emphasise the fact that the superstructure operates retroactively on its base, and that both spheres therefore determine each other. The retroactive superstructural influence is no less important than the influence of the base itself. The historical process can only be explained by observing the interaction of the two. They do not affect each other mechanically or as externally independent factors; they form inseparable moments of a unity.

A particular historical event can only be explained by a whole series of causal factors. Historical materialism does not deny that superstructural factors have an influence; it examines these factors and eventually leads them back to the economic base. It does not regard these factors as accidental but as bound together by necessity, and brings out the decisive economic factor which prevails "in the last instance".

Since the superstructure has a certain autonomy of movement, it does not necessarily correspond completely to the base at every historical moment. The parallels between the two reveal themselves over a long historical period. In some cases there may be tension between them. Political relations may change more slowly than the relations of production; law may only adjust slowly to economic changes. On the other hand, scientific development can precede economic development. When this tension becomes too great in the long term it is relieved, and when the divergences are very marked it is relieved by revolution. The solution to the contradictions of material life (i.e. revolution) does not necessarily achieve adequate expression in the social consciousness of the period; but the ideas with which men conceive of the conflicts of their times form a constituent part of the revolutionary upheaval itself.

The Dialectical Relationship

Clarifying the relation between base and superstructure enables us to understand, in a more concrete way than before, the relation between consciousness and being which was our starting-point. Consciousness coincides with the concept of ideological superstructure, with human ideas. But in addition to this, social being now reveals itself to its fullest extent, in its concrete totality: it is not restricted to the economic base, but embraces the whole superstructure. Consciousness turns out to be a part of this being: more precisely, it is conscious being. The unity of being and consciousness now shows itself to be not a merely external relationship but an inseparable association. By "humanising" the problem of the relation between thought and being, Marx came to recognise being as human and social, not merely natural being, and to recognise consciousness as human thought; this enabled him to demonstrate the unity of both. "Thought and being are indeed *distinct*, but they are also in *unity* with each other." Thought, as a part of human being, no longer plays a merely contemplative role outside the historical process. It becomes itself a fac-

58

tor of historical change. This opens the way to recognition of the dialectical unity of subject and object, and of theory and practice.

The meaning of the statement that social being determines consciousness now becomes clear. Social being does not simply mean economic relations. Economic relations are the foundation of social life and prevail in the last instance. But in any analysis of an individual situation it is social being as a whole that has to be taken into account — the economic and political relations certainly, but also the existing social ideologies and the intellectual tradition. These latter superstructural forces do not act independently of the other factors. They are themselves the expression of certain material relations of production, but relations which are probably already things of the past, which have lost their material reality but have not yet quite discarded their "conscious" expression. When we want to account for the consciousness of a particular human group it is by no means enough to classify them simply in economic terms or to determine their class identity, even if this is where the most important objective (rather than subjective) roots of their actions lie. A precise analysis must take account of all the concrete factors of their social being. What is important is not just the question of which class they belong to but also (for example) the particular layer or role which they occupy within that class, the social position of the family (e.g. the white-collar "proletarian" who comes from a once rich bourgeois family), and above all, the ideological traditions of the group (religion, received political or philosophical ideas and prejudices etc.).

Vulgar marxists of all political tendencies usually neglect these wide-ranging factors of social being. In particular the oscillating political behaviour of the middle layers, who overlap bourgeoisie and proletariat, can only be explained — let alone influenced — if a very careful examination is made of all the essential elements of their social existence. Yet as a rule, this problem is calmly shrugged aside with some cliché about the proletarisation of their economic existence forcing them politically into the ranks of the proletariat. And while the vulgar marxist politicians in Germany wait for the petty bourgeoisie to develop a proletarian class consciousness and become socialists, these layers turn in a mass towards national socialism — a clear indication that "social being" does not simply mean "economic situation". Religion, upbringing, the cultural tradition, political prejudices received in the family environment: all these are social factors, whose importance is no less than that of the economic base.

The relation between consciousness and being can thus only be correctly understood if being is conceived of dynamically, as process. It then loses its rigidly objective form; individual things on the surface of social being are removed from their isolation and seen as processes within the framework of the social totality. When the great basic principle of the dialectic is applied, "the world is not seen as a complex of achieved things but as a complex of processes". Social reality in its historical flux is shown to be human reality, i.e. the totality of human relations rather than a relation between things. Consciousness no longer stands outside being and is no longer separated from its object. It is a moving and moved part of the historical becoming of reality. Consciousness is determined by the transformation of being; but, as the consciousness of acting men, it in turn transforms this being. Consciousness is no longer consciousness *above* an object, the duplicated "reflection" of an individual object, but a constituent part of changing relations, which are what they are only in conjunction with the consciousness that corresponds to their material existence. Consciousness is the self-knowledge of reality, an expression and a part of the historical process of being, which knows itself at every stage of development.

The humanist standpoint enables us to see what Hegel, from the idealist standpoint, could not — that is, a truly dialectical relationship between consciousness and being. Consciousness, as conscious and human being, is "in unity with being and yet distinct from it". The dialectical unity reveals itself in the interaction within the historical dynamic of human reality. This interaction can no longer be seen as the mechanical reciprocal effects of two independent forces, as a purely external relationship: human "being" is now "becoming", and also comprises "consciousness". The concrete expression of this dialectical unity is the unity of theory and practice.

Marxism has been treated in this essay as the scientific theory which it undoubtedly is. But it is more than this. It can be distinguished from all other theories by the fact that it is not a contemplative but a practical theory. The knowledge that consciousness is a part of being demands, of the theory which knows this, that it regard itself as a constituent part of practice, a part of the development of being. Theory and practice form a unity: theory becomes practical theory (the marxist workers' movement), while practice becomes conscious practice, rather than sheer unconscious activity.

Historical materialism does not merely see consciousness as socially determined (non-marxist sociology does this); it also sees consciousness as a factor in changing social reality.

Theory is reality's knowledge of itself. Hegel too saw this; but for him "reality" meant the Idea, which comes to know itself in the course of the historical process. For Marx, on the other hand, reality is human reality, and consciousness human consciousness. Thus the man who knows reality no longer stands outside history like Hegel's "Philosopher" but is himself a factor in transforming social relations. Theory no longer exists merely *post festum* but becomes a lever in the revolutionary process. Dialectical materialism is both the expression and the means of a theoretical critique, "in its essence, a critical and revolutionary method".

Theory is therefore essentially critique. It is no accident that Marx called his major work a *"critique* of political economy". Marxism is a critique of bourgeois economy and ideology from the standpoint of the proletariat. It does not replace it with a new, proletarian "theory" or any other kind of theory: it theoretically *criticises* those bourgeois institutions and ideas which the proletariat attacks and criticises in practice, in the class struggle.

The unity of theory and practice clearly occurs in the union between socialism and the workers' movement; marxist socialism is the theoretical expression of the working-class movement. The union of marxist theoretical critique with the practi-

61

cal-critical activity of the proletariat has a dual form. "Theory becomes material power as soon as it seizes the masses," wrote Marx as early as 1844, in his *Critique of Hegel's "Philosophy of Law"*. Marxist socialism is thus a theory which seeks to be assimilated by the masses; it addresses itself to the proletariat. It is not content with criticising existing relations. The theoretical critique is only a preparation for the practical revolution which forms the "conclusions" of that critique. This is the meaning of Marx's eleventh thesis on Feuerbach — "philosophers have only interpreted the world in various ways, but the point is to change it". There is not the slightest suggestion here that purely contemplative theory should be replaced by activity alone, by a pure practice without theory. Practice must be conscious practice; the critique exists "in human practice and in the comprehension of this practice". In this way the "weapon of critique" becomes "critique in the form of weapons"; theory is translated into practice and accompanies that practice.

The relationship between theory and practice is therefore neither accidental nor external. It is not true that theory first knows something and that practice then applies this knowledge more or less accordingly. Consciousness is a necessary component and a determining element of practice, and a precondition for the transformation of reality. A correct consciousness of existing relations, and the demystification of the appearance and the ideology which they generate, are the necessary preconditions for the revolutionary practice of the proletariat. "These fossilised relations must be made to dance, they must have their own song sung to them," wrote the young Marx in his *Critique of Hegel's "Philosophy of Law"*. In the same way, he spoke of the "reform of consciousness" which must explain to the world its own actions and "shout to it the slogan of its own struggle . . . it will then be seen that the world has for a long time possessed the dream of something, of which it only needs to possess the consciousness in order to possess it in fact." To become conscious is thus the decisive step towards revolutionary practice.

Theory, however, is no mere textbook guide to practice; it is the expression of practice. Marxism undertakes a theoretical critique of all forms of bourgeois ideology, but this is also the "general expression of the actual conditions of an existing class struggle". Since marxism consciously regards itself as the expression of the struggle of a class, it cannot counterpose any "pure science without presuppositions" to the ideology which it is criticising. Its task is to criticise bourgeois ideology by exposing its presuppositions. Bourgeois ideology itself is ignorant of these, for they show this ideology to be the product of one class in a society split into classes; a critique of it is only possible from the standpoint of the struggle of another class and in combination with that struggle. This class is the proletariat, the living critique of the capitalist social order in whose conditions of existence "all the conditions of life of present-day society are summed up in their most inhuman forms". Its critique of bourgeois ideology, therefore, cannot stop at the establishment of a new theory which expresses the point of view of the proletariat. It can only conclude with the practical removal, by the proletariat, of their inhuman conditions of life and the inhuman conditions of life of society as a whole. Only the removal of these can create the foundations of a new, pure knowledge which is no longer determined by class.

This consciousness-making characteristic of practice is the second component in the dual form of the unity between theory and practice. Like all the essential elements of Marx's theory, this question too has been quite distorted by his epigones. I shall refer to just two typical examples. Hilferding wrote in his foreword to *Finance Capital*:

> "The politics of marxism is, like its theory, free from value-judgments. It is therefore false to identify marxism directly with socialism (even though there is a widespread misconception to this effect both *intra* and *extra muros*). For marxism, if it is looked at logically as a scientific system, independent of its historical effects, is simply a theory of the laws of movement of society, formulated in general by the marxist conception of history and applied by marxist economics in the era of commodity production. . . . An understanding of the correctness of marxism and the necessity of socialism is not necessarily a pointer

to practical behaviour."

In the same way, Kautsky wrote that the materialist conception of history is, "as scientific doctrine, in no way connected with the proletariat". It is a "purely scientific doctrine" which is only proletarian inasmuch as it is recognised almost exclusively by the proletariat and its intellectual representatives.

These are by no means isolated examples — they come from two "eminent" marxists. Both of them completely fail to understand Marx's dialectic. Marxism ceases to be "in its essence a critical and revolutionary method" and becomes a reflective science, separated from practice and designed not to change the world but to interpret it. This apparently "scientific" vulgar marxism also "proves" that socialism grows "naturally", that it "must" come about quite independently of human will. This may soothe and convince the philistine spirit in many a worker, but in actual fact it is as unscientific as it could possibly be, a complete distortion of Marx's theory. The fundamental misunderstanding which underlies these notions is their separation of consciousness from its object (and consequently of theory from practice). This separation occurs because they fail to see through the reified appearance of capitalist relations of production, which seem to them to confront man as "natural" relations rather than as the human relations which they actually are.

Marx's concrete application of the dialectic in these questions can only be grasped if we recognise the humanist character of his theory. The conception of social man as the subject-object of knowledge, the conception of being as human being and of consciousness as conscious being: this is the step which turns marxism into a theory of revolution. When Vico wrote that man was capable of knowing the social world because man himself had created it, he was already seeking a way of associating knowledge with transformation. But by locating human consciousness in human reality, Marx showed that knowledge represents a transformation of reality from the very beginning. Theory has become practical; practice, conversely, has become conscious. The way is open towards real knowledge, and towards the accompanying transformation of social life:

"social life", said Marx, "is essentially practical. All mysteries which lead theory to mysticism find their rational solution in human practice and in the comprehension of this practice".

CHAPTER III: Distortion and Renewal by Marx's Followers

The Distortion of the Question by the Epigones

The conception of marxism as humanism is fundamental to our argument. It is a conception which Marx himself developed in his early writings where he roundly criticised "ideology", and which he applied concretely in his critique of political economy. The humanist conception is the key to Marx's treatment of the relation between consciousness and being. His first step was the critique of Hegel: consciousness was recognised as human consciousness, and was located in reality. The second step was the critique of Feuerbach: reality was recognised as human and social, no longer as abstract and natural. In the process of a more detailed consideration of social reality, we have made a methodological classification of its various elements (economic base, political, legal and ideological superstructure), though these elements must be regarded as part of the social totality in the process of transformation, movement, and interaction with each other. At this point the notion of consciousness as conscious being acquires a concrete meaning. The unity of the subject and object of knowledge and the unity of consciousness and being achieve expression in the unity of theory and practice and the association of marxism with the workers' movement. Theory is recognised as the expression of the practical-critical activity of the proletariat. It is, "in its essence, critical and revolutionary" theory, and it leads to the practical removal of the object which it has theoretically criticised, i.e. to the overthrow of the existing relations.

This positive chain of reasoning must now be supplemented by a critique of other presentations of the same problem. One difficulty with all historical materialist writing is that Marx and Engels never published their thoughts on this question in a single consistent context. Their views have to be gathered from a whole number of writings and letters. It is impossible to get an overall picture of the materialist conception of history unless one approaches the sources in the spirit of the authors, using the dialectical method to develop it further. But since this materialist dialectic is only dealt with by Marx and Engels in occasional remarks, to apply it by analogy presupposes that one understands the way in which its two founders applied it, concretely, in their writings (and especially in *Capital*). The problem of how to present historical materialism cannot be solved by the faithful and literal reproduction of quotations. It demands an independent working through, with the help of Marx's *method*. This is a task which is, of course, only for Marx's disciples. Anti-marxist presentations of marxism, even when they manage to talk about essentials, do not use Marx's dialetical materialist method; they dismiss it as "sheer hocus-pocus" or "metaphysical trickery". I shall confine myself to examinations of the problem from the marxist camp, those which by and large are extended developments of Marx's theory. By this same token I shall not deal with the revisionist socialists (e.g. Bernstein, De Man), whose ideas are actually rooted in the bourgeois critique.

Since this book cannot cover all the marxist literature on the subject of historical materialism, I shall discuss three representative tendencies which have developed in the marxist camp and which embrace all the important theoreticians who have dealt with the problem. The first is Karl Kautsky, who as the main theoretical representative of prewar social democracy mediated the theories of Marx and Engels to a whole generation of marxists. The other two tendencies derive from him. One was founded by Plekhanov, became, through the agency of Lenin, the dominant tendency in the Communist International, and "took off" in the postwar period both inside and outside Russia. The other tendency is that which seeks to supplement Marx "critically", with kantian theories. Its chief theoreticians are Braunthal, Woltmann and Vorländer; the object of our critique will be their leader, Max Adler (who is also closer to marxism than they).

In spite of their theoretical and political differences, all these tendencies have a common feature: they abandon Marx's dialectic and consequently fail to understand the humanist character of his theory, though Max Adler occasionally comes close to it. And their distortion of Marx's solution to the problem of consciousness and being is also distinguished by a common feature, which is that theory and practice do not form a real unity, that consciousness is separated from its object and theory from practice. All three tendencies fight each other, bitterly at times. They are truly the struggles of epigones: disciples who, while they do not reach the same theoretical level as the founders of their doctrine, fight among themselves for the privilege of interpreting and developing it.

Karl Kautsky wrote *The Materialist Conception of History* at a time when he was no longer generally recognised as the standard marxist theoretician. Nevertheless, it still typifies the ideas of the Second International both in the prewar period and today. The critical attention which this lengthy work has justifiably received has come for the most part from within the marxist camp. For a pertinent and comprehensive discussion of the book, the reader is referred to Karl Korsch; I shall confine myself to his treatment of the themes we have already touched on.

Kautsky's misunderstanding of Marx's theory stems from his suppression of the dialectic. Kautsky turns the dialectic from a critical and revolutionary method into a mechanical scheme of development; he raises "very considerable cautions" about it, "particularly after the materialist inversion of it". The dialectic is one very general law of development (not the only one) in nature and history; the human mind is conservative and can only be revolutionised by its environment, and the dialectic is therefore simply "the adjusting of thoughts to facts" and "the adjusting of thoughts to each other". This is how Kautsky's section on the dialectic concludes; at the same time he polemicises against Engels's "idealist" version of it. The dialectical relationship between consciousness and being, which Marx saw as "indeed *distinct*, but also in *unity* with each other", does not exist for Kautsky, any more than the dialectical relationship between theory and practice.

It is not surprising that Kautsky's "materialist conception of history" turns out to be natural evolution, not marxist humanism. He sees it as his personal task to extend the materialist conception of history to the sphere of biology. He wonders "whether the development of human societies is not linked internally to that of animal and plant species, with the result that the history of humanity is only a special instance of the history of living creatures, with a particular set of laws derived from living nature". He reaches the conclusion that there is a general law to which human as well as animal and plant evolution is subject, the law "that every transformation of societies, like that of species, is traceable to a transformation of the environment". Marx and Engels, however, saw nature as simply the foundation of social life; their dialectical materialist conception of history found its real sphere of application in historical development. Kautsky's naturalistic materialism directly opposes this theory. His attempt to determine evolution through environmental influence deserves the same reply that Marx gave to contemplative, undialectical materialism in the third thesis on Feuerbach:

"The materialist doctrine concerning the transformation of circumstances and upbringing forgets that circumstances are changed by men and that it is essential to educate the educator himself. This doctrine, therefore, necessarily divides society into two parts, one of which is superior to society.

The coincidence of the transformation of circumstances and of human activity or self-transformation can be conceived and rationally understood only as *revolutionary practice*."

Kautsky, however, is a long way from this revolutionary practice. As a result of his non-humanist, naturalistic materialism, he is forced to oppose "mind and matter" to each other, and thus to separate consciousness from being. He may state that the two of them "interact" externally, but this in no way alters his conception. Marx's unity of thought and being, which proceeds from the existence of human consciousness in human, social reality, obviously cannot be bracketed with Kautsky's brand of materialism, which belongs to the natural sciences.

There is a philosophical dualism in Kautsky which contradicts its own natural-science based materialism. It cannot be removed simply by observing that "there is no mind in itself, independent of particular bodies", or that "social and thus mental connections between thinking men belong to the environment which we call 'material'". This is a long way from Marx's conception of consciousness as nothing but conscious being, and the being of man as his actual life process.

When we compare Kautsky's conception of the relation between theory and practice with Marx's, we find that Kautsky simply does not mention the unity between them which Marx posed so concisely in the *Theses on Feuerbach*. On the relation between knowledge and action, he states instead that in order to act in a systematic way, the human organism has first of all to be able to distinguish what is in the environment. The unity of theory and practice is reduced to the idea that man's knowledge of previous history may teach him to make future history. Historical materialism's other task, according to Kautsky, is to furnish man with the scientific knowledge which will enable him "to find his orientation in the surrounding and threatening environment". It is scarcely possible to imagine a more striking contrast to Marx's final thesis on Feuerbach, that the point is not (passively) to interpret the world but (actively) to change it.

Lenin's ideas on this subject, and those of his own followers, are not so far removed from Kautsky's. Lenin's point of departure, like Kautsky's, is not human society but nature:

> "Materialism recognises in a general way that real, objective being (matter) is independent of the consciousness, sensations, experience etc. of man. Historical materialism recognises that social being is independent of the social consciousness of man."[18]

While Marx proceeds from "social matter", i.e. from social relations, Lenin proceeds from matter in its "philosophical" sense:

> "Materialism, in full agreement with natural science, accepts matter as the primary *datum* and consciousness, thought, sensation as secondary."

70

This is a superb example of the metaphysical materialism which Hegel described in the *Phenomenology of Mind* as the complementary aspect of theism, i.e. precisely the theism which Lenin always fought against so keenly. Marx quotes this remark of Hegel's with approval in *The Holy Family*; in another passage in the same book he condemns the kind of view which Lenin was later to put forward, stating that speculative and every other kind of metaphysics had "succumbed forever to the [dialectical] kind of materialism which coincides with humanism".

Because matter is the foundation of Lenin's theory, consciousness loses its reality and becomes an attribute of matter, which alone is real; consciousness becomes the mere duplicated reflection of matter. Lenin, along with Diderot, looks at "sensation as one of the attributes of matter in movement. . . Sensation, thought, consciousness are the highest products of matter organised in a particular way. . . . Our sensations, our consciousness are only the reflection of the external world, and it is self-evident that a reflection cannot exist without what is reflected, while what is reflected can exist without that which is reflecting it". Consciousness, which for Marx was "conscious being", has become an attribute, a reflection, a mere duplicate of matter.

Since Lenin does not regard being as human, consciousness can no longer be "in unity with it". Lenin's naturalistic, metaphysical materialism thus leads to an absolute separation of consciousness from being. He arrives at a theory of knowledge which is still limited to the relation between the subject and object of knowledge; he thus lapses back into Hegel's idealist "unity" of the two, which is in fact an absolute dualism betwen thought and being, mind and matter. There is an Absolute Truth, which we approach in an "endless, ongoing evolutionary process that is basically without contradictions".

The following remarks show with particular clarity how little Lenin understands the unity of consciousness and being in man:

"Consciousness in general *reflects* being — this is the general thesis of *all* materialism. It is impossible to avoid seeing its *inseparable* connection with the historical mate-

rialist thesis: social consciousness *reflects* social being."[19]
Lenin's theory of reflection clearly opposes consciousness to its
object. What chiefly indicates this is the highly revealing reference to the concept of "social consciousness", which Lenin
uses here and elsewhere in contrast to Marx's "social being".
One must assume that when Lenin used two different expres-
sions, "consciousness" and "social consciousness", he was
not intending to contrast the thought of the individual with
social thought. The only possible assumption, therefore, is that
by "social consciousness" he in fact means human consciousness, and that the consciousness which reflects being in general is therefore a supra-human consciousness, a kind of "pure
Idea", i.e. Hegel's Self-consciousness. Of course, Lenin does not
in the least intend to say this. But this small example shows
how far he has been led astray by his undialectical confusion
of Marx's dialectical and social materialism ("which coincides
with humanism") with metaphysical, naturalistic materialism.

This metaphysical materialism is of course incapable of the
results which Marx's conception produces, i.e. the unity of
theory and practice. According to Luppol, the "unity of theory
and practice" signifies a practice which is "conscious" (i.e.
theoretically elaborated), and a theory which is translated into
practice. Deborin, Lenin's faithful interpreter, wrote that "the
real unity of theory and practice is realised by the practical
transformation of reality, by the revolutionary movement,
which bases itself on the theortically discovered laws of development of reality".[20] In both these notions, theory is clearly regarded as contemplative: the relationship of theory to practice lies in the fact that theory can be "applied". Hilferding
and Kautsky believe that marxism has no *necessary* association
with the workers' movement; for Lenin, it is a theory which
the workers' movement *can* apply. In neither case is theory
the conscious expression of the revolutionary practice of the
proletariat. It is no longer a constituent part of reality, a theory
which transforms that reality from the beginning, by transforming human consciousness, and which concludes with the
practical overthrow of the reality that is theoretically criticised.

Max Adler is representative of the tendency which seeks to base

72

its marxism on the "critique of knowledge". He comes closer than Kautsky or the leninists to the standpoint of this book. I shall not give a detailed account of the philosophical basis of his view, except where it concerns the question of consciousness and being. Adler's critique of the naturalistic, metaphysical materialism of Lenin and Kautsky has a certain validity. He realises, correctly, that this philosophical version of materialism has nothing to do with marxism, which sees its object as society, not nature.

When Adler states that Marx's theory is a "humanisation of economic relations"[21] he gets very close to the humanist solution to the question of consciousness and being. But his kantian, critical-idealist standpoint prevents him from recognising the dialectic in this relationship. He is forced to draw a sharp dividing-line between thought and being. Thus he separates the dialectic "as a mere mode of thought" from the dialectic "as a real state of opposition within the being of things themselves". Engels says that these two forms of the dialectic are "two series of laws which are basically identical". But Adler has created this thoroughly undialectical opposition between consciousness and being: he is forced to call the first of the two forms "dialectic" and the second "antagonism", and to locate the process of interaction purely within the realm of consciousness. He does this by stating, first, that since economic relations are human relations they are *also* "spiritual relations", relations of mind [*geistige Verhältnisse*], and then that they are *only* relations of mind: "Economy, like ideology, is something of the mind. It is simply another form of mind."

With this he proceeds to "spiritualise" [*vergeistigen*] social being, a step which he justifies in the following way:

"This social being is something more than the mere natural being of things. For Marx, consciousness is from the beginning inserted into a process which is no longer exactly a simple natural process but rather a social process. This latter, however, is impossible without the activity of men, conscious of their goal."

From this quite correct beginning, Adler reaches the curious conclusion that consciousness "is in no way determined by anything alien to it", since social being is "something spiritual".

73

This allows him to argue the unity of economy and ideology, which "in a spiritual coherence" comprise the unity of social life. The mutual dependence of both these spheres on each other is "the dependence of one form of the spiritual on another".

Adler proceeds from the correct assumption that a "spiritual" element or element of mind is contained in economic relations, since they are relations entered into by thinking men; but it is a manifest fallacy for him to then describe these relations as *purely* relations of mind. It is certainly true that without "the appropriate activity of man" the social process is impossible, but it does not in the least follow that this social process *only* exists in consciousness. Adler makes the equally fallacious deduction that Marx and Engels "regard and define economic relations completely as spiritual relations"; he quotes a passage from *The German Ideology* in which the connection between the "production of ideas" and material production is made with particular emphasis.

Marx states here that "consciousness can only be conscious being, and the being of men is their actual life process"; but it seems impossible to extract from this any indication that being is to be seen purely as something "spiritual". Marx himself spoke out explicitly against any such interpretation:

"Communist workers know full well that property, capital, money, wage labour etc. are in no way the mere creations of their imagination but are the extremely concrete and practical results of their own self-alienation, and must be removed in a concrete and practical way if man is to become man not only in thought, in consciousness, but also in mass being, in life."[22]

Adler's "spiritualised" theory remains purely reflective, not practical. He complains about scientific marxism getting entangled with politics, and defines marxism as science, as sociology. He describes the relation of science to politics in marxism as follows. Marxism attempts to achieve a scientific understanding of social life as "social practice, to illuminate it from within"; in this way it reaches an understanding of the past and a "knowledge of the necessary goal in the future". Political activity is a result of this theory, never its precondition. Having

74

made this neat kantian separation of theoretical from practical behaviour, Adler terms the whole thing "unity of theory and practice", and says that the concrete expression of this unity is "the conscious execution of social legality". He does not regard consciousness as a moment of reality, as "conscious being" in which the transformation of the content of consciousness has a direct practical effect; he regards consciousness as contemplative, as standing basically outside reality. One recognises a social legality and one obeys it, instead of seeing oneself as a part of the recognised reality, as incorporating one's own actions into this legality and transforming it. What Marx said in the first thesis on Feuerbach is true also of Adler: "reality, sensuousness, is conceived only in the form of the *object*, or of *contemplation*, but not as *sensuous human activity*, not as *practice*" (in spite of Adler's use of this term), "not *subjectively*". He fails to comprehend the significance of revolutionary, practical-critical activity. Marx's description of the relation of his theory to the revolutionary activity of the working class in *The Communist Manifesto* is in complete opposition to Adler:

> "The theoretical conceptions of the communists are simply the general expression of the actual conditions of an existing class struggle, of a historical movement which is going on under our noses."

The Beginnings of Renewal

The three basic theoretical tendencies which describe themselves as marxist have in fact distorted Marx's solution to the problem of the relation between being and consciousness. Both Kautsky and Lenin tended to overlook the application of historical materialism to its own actual domain, i.e. social life; they failed to understand its humanist character and turned it into a naturalistic materialism. Adler's brand of distortion was to "spiritualise" material relations. The common result of both forms of distortion is that they regard marxism essentially as a contemplative theory. This leads them to make an absolute separation of consciousness from being and of theory from practice, though they all orthodoxly cloak this separation

75

with the totally unjustified term "unity".

In the face of this theoretical decline of marxism at the hands of its most eminent representatives there are only two theoreticians who have restored the critical and revolutionary character of Marx's doctrine in such a way as to nourish its further development: Georg Lukács and Karl Korsch. Lukács represents a tendency whose adherents (including Révai and Fogarasi) have capitulated to the attacks against their positions made by the Communist International. These were not simply theoretical attacks but took the form of intense pressures, and they no longer defend their standpoint. Korsch, on the other hand, is representative of the political tendency which criticised and fought back "from the left" against the theoretical and practical opportunism of the Communist International from which it came.

Both tendencies set out by trying to defend and restore the real sense of Marx's theory. They succeed by applying the theory only as a means of taking it further. In Korsch this takes the form of a critique of the rigidified and purely formal marxist "orthodoxy" of the prevailing marxist tendencies, a critique which demonstrates both why the theoretical degeneration took place and how it can be overcome. Lukács, on the other hand, pays particular attention to the restoration of Marx's dialectic. In so doing, he brings out the essential features of this dialectic which, although applied in practice by Marx in all his writings, are almost nowhere given a methodological treatment and which are totally neglected by Engels. By bringing to light some of the almost completely forgotten basic problems which Marx dealt with (reification, for example), whose crucial importance was only revealed when the early writings were eventually published, Lukács opened up a whole new and important field of work for marxism in the study of reification and the problem of ideology.

In his two books *Marxism and Philosophy* and *The Materialist Conception of History: A Debate with Karl Kautsky*, Karl Korsch makes a detailed examination of how marxist theory has degenerated, especially in Kautsky and (with the second edition of *Marxism and Philosophy*) in "marxism-leninism".

He recognises marxist theory as the general expression of the concrete historical conditions for the practice of the working-class movement. In the light of this, he asserts that the acceptance of marxism by the international workers' movement towards the end of the nineteenth century was purely formal and "ideological". In reality, it "only accepted, even in theory, isolated economic, political and social theories torn from the context of the revolutionary marxist totality; their general meaning was therefore changed, and their particular content falsified and mutilated".[23] This purely formal acceptance is accounted for by the fact that "the workers' movement of that time . . . even though its actual practice was on a broader basis than before, had remained below the heights which the revolutionary movement as a whole and the class struggle of the proletariat had previously reached in its general and theoretical development, during the closing phase of capitalism's first cycle of historical development (which came to an end around the middle of the century)". What Korsch says here about the "marxism of the Second International" is equally true of the Third, which developed out of the particularly "orthodox" Russian marxism of the prewar period. These two tendencies, together with Adler's kantian-marxist tendency, constitute the "new historical form of the proletarian class theory" which "has emerged from the changed practical conditions of the class struggle in a new historical epoch".

From the special problem of "marxism and philosophy", by way of the new "third period of development of marxism which began at the turn of the century", Korsch reaches the problem of the relation between consciousness and being, and criticises the "primitive, pre-dialectical and even pre-transcendental conceptions" of this relation which dominate all the main tendencies of marxism referred to above. His conclusions tally with the viewpoint of this book, and I shall therefore limit myself to confirming this with a few characteristic references.

Korsch criticises the leninist conception for wrongly "shifting the dialectic unilaterally into the Object, nature and history" and for "ascribing the knowledge of this objective being to subjective consciousness". He contrasts this with the materialist dialectic of Marx and Engels, "who see the question as one of the relation between the whole of historical being and all historical forms of consciousness". In other words, he recognises the humanist character of Marx's theory. He correctly understands "the coincidence of consciousness and reality", which lies in the fact that consciousness is not in opposition to reality but exists "in this world, as an actual and real part of this natural and historical, social world (even if it is an 'ideal' part)". This enables him to reassert the unity of theory and practice. Korsch criticises Lenin's "quite abstract opposition of pure theory, which discovers truths, to pure practice, which applies these discovered truths to reality". In contrast to this conception, and with the aid of Marx's *Theses on Feuerbach*, Korsch develops the "principle of the new, dialectical materialist method":

> "Theoretical critique and practical revolution are inseparably linked activities — not in any abstract sense of the expression, but as the concrete and real transformation of the concrete and real world of bourgeois society."

Korsch thus establishes the necessity of the connection between marxist theory and the workers' movement, which he formulates as follows:

> "The birth of marxist theory is, to speak in hegelian marxist terms, simply the 'other side' of the birth of the actual proletarian class movement; both sides together are what forms the concrete totality of the historical process."

The most important thing about Georg Lukács's much debated book *History and Class Consciousness* is its presentation of the dialectic. I shall only deal with it here, like the other works to which I have referred, in the light of its approach to the problem of consciousness and being.

Lukács begins by confirming the materialist dialectic as "in its essence, a critical and revolutionary method". The unity of theory and practice, by which theory becomes "the vehicle of the revolution", can only be a real unity if the moment of becoming conscious is closely linked with action, so that it also constitutes a decisive step towards the practical process of revolution. This necessitates the dialectical unity of the subject and object of knowledge in the historical process, and the unity of human, social being and human consciousness. The natural economic laws which seem to be independent of man are shown to be mere reified appearance; social reality is something which can be known and transformed, as human practice.

The precondition for this is fulfilled by the emergence in history of the proletariat. The theory which expresses this unity of theory and practice is, "essentially, nothing but the expression in thought of the revolutionary process itself". It is the class consciousness of the proletariat, more precisely, which fulfils the precondition. This class consciousness breaks through capitalist reification and recognises "economic" factors as relationships between man and society in their concrete totality. Full knowledge of reality enables the proletariat to grasp its own role in that reality, which is to transform these relations. Class consciousness acquires a practical form in the revolutionary party, whose role is "to be bearers of the class consciousness of the proletariat, the 'conscience' of its historical mission". The practical significance of theory finds its clearest expression in the party, the lever of social revolution.

Lukács clearly brings out the humanist character of the dialectic, especially its role in removing the reified appearance of social relations. Some of his critics, however, accuse him of idealism, since he applies the dialectic only to society and not to nature, and thus draws a dividing-line between the two spheres which does not exist in Marx. Nowhere in Lukács is there a consistent account of the relation between nature and society. The most explicit reference comes in his statement that "for marxists, as historical dialecticians, nature and all forms of its theoretical and practical conquest are social categories", not supra-social or supra-historical ones.

This denial of a supra-temporal importance to natural science, or of any independence from class considerations, comes as a shock to the leninist critic Rudas, who complains that in Lukács's thesis "there can be found no tool with which to establish the objectivity of a truth". For the leninists, as we have already seen, this objective truth is a kind of "thing in itself" which is strictly distinct from human knowledge and which can be merely approached, in a process of never ending

79

approximation to knowledge. Lukács's conception, however, is quite in accord with that of Marx and Engels, who would not have approved of Lenin's separation of consciousness from being, and who see nature as "socialised" nature, modified by men. But the accusation against Lukács is justifiable to the extent that he uses the dialectical method incidentally to draw conclusions about the concrete formation of reality, instead of seeing it as the abstract *expression* of that reality.

Lukács sharply attacks the "theory of reflection", which he sees as the theoretical objectification of a duality between consciousness and reality, thought and being. He regards it as an expression of bourgeois, reified consciousness, which believes that it knows reality when what it is actually seeing is only the reified, surface appearance of reality, where human relationships appear as the relationships of things to each other. The rigidity of this objective appearance of the capitalist world forces reality to disintegrate into individual objects which consciousness appears to confront independently.

Lukács shows us the really fertile significance of humanism, which is its role in the dissolution of reification, of that "self-alienation of man" (Marx) which under capitalism is the central category of consciousness and is at the root of ideologies. The class consciousness of the proletariat represents the removal of this reification.

FALSE AND CORRECT CONSCIOUSNESS

CHAPTER IV: Alienation and Reification

The Self-alienation of Man and Commodity Fetishism

The central importance of the division of labour in the historical materialist system has already been stressed in chapter two of this book. It is the separation of mental from physical labour that permits the existence of a consciousness which believes itself to be independent of material factors. Ideology, i.e. false consciousness, originates from this circumstance. Let us look more closely at the question of false consciousness. The problematic of an entire scientific discipline, the sociology of knowledge, derives from the fact that capitalist relations appear to the observer not in their real form but in a disguised form. Only this fact can explain how the various scientific conceptions about social reality under capitalism, about its economy, its state, its cultural phenomena, come about.

All divisions of labour until now can be described as natural ones, in the sense that they have occurred independently of man's will, without being consciously regulated or controlled. This natural division of labour means that the individual interests of the members of society diverge from the general interest, and that the deployment of activity is not determined voluntarily but by circumstances apparently independent of man. Man's own activity thus becomes an alien force which confronts and enslaves him, instead of being controlled by him.

The relations of production, i.e. relationships between men in the production of their means of subsistence, appear to be supra-human, natural relations, upon which man is dependent. Each member of society has a particular and exclusive field of activity to which he is tied. Everyone, within the framework of social production as a whole, has to take on a partial function which denies him an overview of the whole context of production. In contrast to the communist mode of production, in which the results of production as a whole are pre-planned, the overall results of social production in all previous stages is neither calculated nor calculable in advance.

Under capitalism, needs are matched with consumption by bringing individual supply into contact with individual demand on the market, which belatedly balances the two. This "balancing" often takes the scarcely "rational" form of crisis. Where the division of labour takes this form, the individual producer can clearly have no overview of the whole process and its functioning. The economic crisis strikes him as a kind of natural catastrophe and certainly not as a product of human activity, which he is inclined to see as being primarily rational. The point is, of course, that this rationality has in the past only existed in the activity of individuals, and has certainly not formed the basis of social processes. In all social formations till now, man's own activity has been alien to him. It seems to him to be the work of higher powers, which he endows with various names in the course of historical development. (Methodologically speaking, it is only a short step from the worship of nature gods to saying that sunspots are the cause of economic crises.) In Marx's terminology this phenomenon is known as the self-alienation of man, or the alienation of labour.

All human labour is linked to a particular means of labour or production, and what distinguishes man from the animals is that he manufactures these means of production. As the division of labour develops, the means of production increasingly acquire the appearance of economic autonomy. In primitive modes of production, the dependence of production on its natural conditions is so great that men represent these to themselves in the form of gods of the earth, fire, fertility, etc. Then, with the social development of technology, the means of production manufactured by man himself takes on the appearance of objects dominating him. Under capitalism the machine, which is actually a tool in the hands of man, develops its own autonomous set of economic laws. The mode of labour of men is adapted to the need to extract value from the machines on which they work. The capitalist market economy, the developed form of commodity production, separates the producer from his product. In all previous forms of production it was production for individual need which predominated; this is now

84

fully displaced by commodity production, i.e. production for an undetermined circle of purchasers.

There is not only a divergence between producer and consumer: the actual producer, the worker, does not manufacture commodities for himself but for the owner of the means of production on which he is occupied. The division of labour reaches a peak. Under feudalism the serf still has his own piece of land and the necessary tools as means of labour; he is able to use a part of his labour power for himself, while the lord of the manor receives the rest. The modern worker, under capitalism, is completely separated from the means of production. He is forced to sell his labour power, his only property, in order to be able to exploit its value as alien means of production. His labour power, i.e. he himself, thus becomes a commodity. "Labour", wrote Marx, "does not only produce commodities; it produces itself and the worker as a commodity — and does so in the proportion in which it produces commodities generally."

Not only the means of labour but the product of his labour become alien to the producer; the object which his labour produces, his product, confronts him as an alien being, as a "power independent of the producer". The product of labour, the incorporation of it into an object, is its *realisation*. For the worker, however, it is also the stripping away [*Entäusserung*] of his labour power, i.e. his *derealisation*. The appropriation of the product of labour, carried out not by the worker but by the capitalist, is an alienation of labour:

> "The worker puts his life into the object; but now his life no longer belongs to him but to the object. Hence, the greater this activity, the greater is the worker's lack of objects. Whatever the product of his labour is, he is not. Therefore the greater this product, the less is he himself. The alienation of the worker in his product does not only mean that his labour becomes an object, an external existence, but that it exists outside him, independently, as something alien to him, and that it becomes a power of its own confronting him; it means that the life which he has conferred on the object confronts him as something hostile and alien."[24]

This alienation of labour reveals itself in various forms. Firstly, the product of labour is an object alien to the worker, dominating him. He does not control the machine: capital, i.e. the economic substance of this machine, dominates him. Capital, this social relation of production, necessarily appears to him to be an alien and, as it were, natural power. The alienation of labour expresses itself further in the fact that labour is not a natural need to which the worker submits, but simply a means of meeting the needs of his existence: "his labour is therefore not voluntary but coerced; it is *forced* labour. . . . Its alien character emerges clearly in the fact that as soon as no physical or other compulsion exists, labour is shunned like the plague. . . . The external character of labour for the worker appears in the fact that it is not his own but someone else's. . . . It is the loss of his self."[25]

Since production is the expression of the social life of men, and since the product is therefore the objectification of this social existence, the alienation of labour has the effect of an alienation of man from man. Social life becomes merely a means for man's self-preservation. He is under the impression that he can only live alone, and does not directly sense himself to be a part of human society. There is a divergence between his personal fate and the common fate. This alienation of man from his labour and of man from man is the root of individualism, which imagines that society somehow originated "on the quiet" by voluntary consent of the individual members, without realising that these individuals would not exist if it were not for society and that they are determined by society in the first place. As the capitalist economic order develops, this circumstance is intensified by increasing specialisation in the production process. The more specialised the partial function of the individual, the less his opportunity of seeing the whole context, thus the more alien to him becomes his labour. The unprecedented specialisation of the sciences and the accompanying loss of knowledge of the totality are further evidence of this.

As capitalism brings all social contradictions to a head and thus makes them visible and recognisable, the phenomenon of self-alienation becomes clearly visible for the first time:

"In all earlier relations of production the domination of men by the conditions of production is no less than in capitalism, but they are concealed by the relations of domination and servitude, which appear and are seen to be the direct motive power of the process of production."[26]

In fact the conditions of production rule the producers in the ancient economy and in the feudal one. The point is, however, that these conditions are mainly factors of nature — weather conditions, for example, which determine the harvest. The increased control over these *natural* conditions of production and the replacement of direct dependence on them by an ever-increasing dependence on *social* conditions of production, makes it possible under capitalism actually to perceive this phenomenon.

Self-alienation affects all classes in bourgeois society, though of course in different ways. Both worker and capitalist are subordinate to the accumulation of capital:

"The possessing class and the class of the proletariat present the same human self-alienation. But the former class feels at home in this self-alienation, it finds confirmation of itself and recognises in alienation *its own power*: it has in it a *semblance* of human existence, while the class of the proletariat feels annihilated in its self-alienation; it sees therein its own powerlessness and the reality of an inhuman existence."[27]

It is precisely this "inhuman existence" of the proletariat that forms one of the elements in the removal of this self-alienation, in the self-realisation of man by means of the revolutionary action of the proletariat. But the road towards this action is a long one, and an essential precondition is correct consciousness and the recognition of these relations of production.

Human self-alienation under capitalism is most clearly expressed by commodity fetishism. The distinguishing feature of the capitalist economy is the fact that it is a pure commodity economy, based on the exchange of goods that are individually appropriated but produced by and for society. Under capitalism, social wealth appears as a vast collection of commodities. The commodity is therefore the root phenomenon of the capitalist economy and also of its ideological superstructure. It was therefore no arbitrary choice that Marx made when he began *Capital*, that critique of bourgeois economy, with his analysis of the commodity. In all earlier forms of production the goods produced usually served consumption directly. Under capitalism, however, they take the form of commodities and thus develop their own autonomous laws, by which their character as use-value retreats behind their economic exchange-value. In every form of natural economy it is the heterogeneity, the quality of the product which is decisive; in the social production of capitalism, this is replaced by the quantitative aspect.

Since use-values appear, without exception, in the form of commodities, the commodity form seems to be necessarily linked to them. The commodity appears to be a constituent part of every economic structure. Capitalism does not primarily produce objects for use but commodities, which simultaneously happen to have the attribute of meeting certain needs. Production proceeds from the rational commercialisation of the commodity, not from the meeting of needs. This is the only way we can account for the fact that, in spite of the existence of unsatisfied needs, whole quantities of goods are sometimes destroyed because they cannot be commercially exploited.

The exchange-value of goods on a social scale is based on their equivalence as products of abstract human labour, which is expressed as the quantitative value of the product of labour. Thus the relations of the producers to each other, objectified in production, assume the appearance of social relations between the products of labour, i.è. of social relations between commodities. The relations of production — *human* relations of domination and servitude — achieve expression in the relations of exchange, and assume the appearance of relationships between commodities with their own autonomous laws.

This extends to the point where human labour power itself is sold directly as a commodity. Service and labour contracts in bourgeois lawbooks are no different from contracts which concern the sale and purchase of objects. Modern labour law is based on recognition of the fact that, in spite of the formal equality of the parties to the contract (which is also true for contracts of sale and purchase), the employee in reality depends on the employer. The price of labour, like that of any other commodity, depends on supply and demand. The very use of the term "labour market" shows that labour alienates man, that labour power has become a thing:

> "The relation of the producers to the sum total of their own labour is presented to them as a social relation of objects which exists outside them. . . . It is a particular social relation between men themselves which in their eyes assumes the phantasmagorical form of a relation between things. . . . This is what I call fetishism: it attaches itself to the products of labour as soon as they are produced as commodities, and it is therefore inseparable from the production of commodities."[28]

The production of objects for use takes place in the piece-meal form of private labour, but for social consumption; the social character of labour, therefore, only appears at the point when the products of labour are exchanged. The commodity now assumes the character of a fetish: it makes what are social relations between persons appear to be relations between things. It appears to the producers that "the social relationships between one private individual and another are not direct social relationships between people at work but, as in fact they are, material relations between people and social relations between things". In the same way,

> "Productive forces appear as a world for themselves, quite independent of and cut off from individuals, alongside the individuals; the reason for this is that the individuals, whose forces they are, are split and in opposition to each other, while these forces on the other hand are only real forces when they are in intercourse and association with these individuals. Thus . . . we have a totality of productive forces which have, as it were, taken on a material form and are for the individuals no longer the forces of the individuals but private property, and hence of the individuals in so far as they are owners of private property themselves."[29]

This is why individuals are obliged to recognise each other primarily as private owners and legal subjects. The worker appears as the private owner of the commodity labour power and sells himself, as a thing, along with that labour power. The alienation of labour is thus a double process: first the powers of man and the products of labour are separated from their human creators, and then they are endowed with their own autonomy. The consequence is that man is ruled by the material form of his own labour.

The commodity-fetish appearance of social relations exists only under capitalism, the developed commodity economy. Under feudalism, social relationships are based on personal dependence:

"But for this very reason . . . there is no necessity for labour and its products to assume a fantastic form different from their reality. They appear as services in kind and payments in kind. . . . No matter, then, what we may think of the parts played by the different classes of people themselves in [feudal] society, the social relations between individuals in the performance of their labour appear at all events as their own mutual personal relations, and are not disguised under the shape of social relations between things, between the products of labour."[30]

The same would also be true of "a union of free men carrying on their labour with the means of production in common, in which the labour power of all the various individuals is consciously applied as the combined labour power of the community". It is in capitalist commodity production alone that the false appearance is a general phenomenon. Since the economy "in the last instance" determines the whole of social life, this fetishism is the central phenomenon in the whole structure of bourgeois society and bourgeois consciousness, where it takes the general form of reification.

Reification in Base and Superstructure

As part of a debate on Marx's *Critique of Political Economy* in the London newspaper *Das Volk* in 1859, Engels stated:

"Economy does not deal with things but with relations between people and, in the last instance, between classes; but these relations are constantly bound up with things and appear as things."

This "reified" appearance is not inherent in the economy alone: it reveals itself in the whole structure of bourgeois society and consciousness.

We have already seen that in the first place, the deciding factor in the manufacture of a commodity is not its quality but its profitability. The importance of the commodity lies in its exchange-value, not its use-value. (This does not necessarily exclude the fact that in order to be exchanged the commodity must also have a use-value.) The costing of the commodity precedes its manufacture and accompanies it on its journey through the world of the economy. Cost calculation, rationalisation: these are the principles of the capitalist economy. The worker (i.e. the commodity labour power) is, like the material means of production, an object to be calculated. The productivity of his labour is calculated in the same way as the productivity of a machine. The work process itself is "rationally" mechanised, broken down into specific psychological phases (the Taylor system), and registered statistically. Rationalised labour in the modern factory is distinguished from handicraft manufacture by the fact that it is broken down into individual actions, partial processes which are executed systematically and are largely independent of each other. The division of labour reaches a point where the product of the partial process becomes itself a commodity, even though it does not yet have the form of an end product, an actual use-value. The qualitative unity of the product is replaced by calculative unity and by the assembly of partial systems which are almost independent of each other.

The quantitative increase in the division of labour which already existed in the handicraft process undergoes a qualitative change. Where there is a division of labour within one factory and between individual factories, any connection between the different partial operations seems to be coincidental. The artisan manufactures a whole or at least sees something emerge by means of an organic division and reintegration of labour, on the basis of an empirical experience of the labour process. But as labour becomes more individual and specialised, the worker loses his overview of the totality of the manufactured end-product. The more the worker lacks an overview of the production of his object as a whole, the less likely is it that in his factory the end-product is manufactured at all; and the employer cannot keep track of the whole of the economic process any more than the worker can. The worker is confronted with a whole labour process to which he must adjust and subordinate himself, knowing neither what came before nor what is to happen afterwards: he must adapt to the movement of the assembly line, which moves independently of his will and dictates the rhythm of his interventions. The individual employer, by the same token, is confronted by the laws of economic life, over which he has no complete view; and since they express the alienation of labour, they necessarily seem to him to be natural laws, independent of man.

The impression which both worker and employer have of being confronted by a process independent of man is reinforced by the increasingly contemplative character of labour. In the running of a modern, rationalised factory the worker's activity tends more and more to consist of observing and regulating the machine. The real representative of the labour process seems to be no longer the working man but the machine. Like a mechanical part, the worker is integrated into a pre-existing labour process over which he has no influence. The special quality of his work becomes less and less important, and is levelled down. Labour becomes abstract labour, measurable only in quantitative terms. (An example of this is the increase in modern industry in the numbers of "semi-skilled" as opposed to "skilled" workers.)

According to Marx, the subordination of man to the machine produces a state of affairs where

> "men are effaced by their labour; the pendulum of the clock has become as accurate a measure of the relative activity of two workers as it is of the speed of two locomotives. Therefore we should not say that one man's hour is worth another man's hour, but rather that one man during an hour is worth just as much as another man during an hour. Time is everything, man is nothing; he is, at the most, time's carcase. Quality no longer matters.

Quantity alone decides everything; hour for hour, day for day."[31]

The machine, far from lightening the worker's labour, confronts him "as capital, as dead labour, which dominates and sucks dry the living labour power. . . . In the factory there exists a lifeless mechanism independent of the worker, who is *annexed* to it as its living appendage".

"Dead labour", capital, dominates not only the worker but the capitalist himself. Of course the latter can regulate the labour process in his own factory, or merge several enterprises into combines and trusts. But he is just as impotent in the face of the total economic process as the individual worker is in the face of the process in his particular factory. He observes the economy and examines its conjunctural cycles in order to adjust to them. But it is precisely these cycles which demonstrate that the social relations which they express remain alien to him, and are not controlled by him. The material form of labour — its product, the commodity — appears to be the real motive factor.

Capital, which in fact is an exploitative social relation between worker and capitalist, appears as a thing, as produced means of production. This capital appears to generate surplus value directly, in the form of interest. "How long ago did economy discard the physiocratic illusion that rents grow out of the soil and not out of society?" asked Marx. Yet capitalism maintains its own equivalent illusion, in the fetishism inherent in capital:

"In the form of interest-bearing capital this appears directly, unaided by the processes of production and circulation. Capital appears to be a mysterious and self-generating form of interest — the source of its own increase. The *thing* (money, commodity, value) is now capital even when it is a mere thing, and capital itself appears as a mere thing. The result of the entire process of reproduction appears as a property inherent in a thing. . . . In interest-bearing capital, therefore, this automatised fetish, self-generating value, money creating money, emerges in its pure state. . . . The social relation is consummated in the relation of a thing, money, to itself. . . . It becomes a property of money to generate value and yield interest, much as it is a property of pear-trees to yield pears. . . . While interest is only a portion of the profit, i.e. of the surplus-value, which the functioning capitalist squeezes out of the worker, it appears now, on the contrary, as though interest were the typical product of capital, the primary matter, and as though profit, in the shape of the profit of the enterprise, were a mere accessory and by-product of the process of reproduction. Hence capital as fetish, hence the fetishism of capital."[32]

The circulation process appears to be the real domain of the economy. This phenomenon also occurs in law, which is essentially law for the circulation of commodities (civil and commercial law and, more recently, legal control over production by means of labour law and economic legislation).

The phenomenon of reification does not only affect the economic base but runs through the whole of social life under capitalism. The break with the old organic forms, and their replacement by rational, calculable relationships, occurs everywhere. Max Weber draws attention to the similarity between the modern state and the economic enterprise:

"The modern state, looked at from the sociological point of view, is an 'enterprise', just as the factory is; this is precisely what is historically specific to it. . . . The modern capitalist enterprise is based, internally, on calculation above all. For its existence it needs forms of 'justice' and management whose functioning may be, at least in principle, rationally calculated according to firm general norms, in the same way that one calculates beforehand the productivity of a machine."[33]

We have already dealt with the correlation between the commodity form and the formal equality of legal subjectivity. Under capitalism, the generality of legal form, the displacement of all organic, traditional relationships by "rational", legally regulated ones, is an expression of reification. It manifests itself everywhere. Patriarchal relationships between master and journeyman in the factory are replaced by the "rational", highly regulated ones between employer and

94

worker; in social life, religious forms of education, marriage, etc., are replaced by legal ones. The dissolution of traditional entities such as the corporations and estates places individuals alongside each other as independent, private persons whose social links take mainly legal forms. The general appearance under capitalism of social relations as legal relations is an expression of reification.

Reification, furthermore, gives rise to particular forms of social consciousness. The appearance of social laws as natural ones which seem to be independent of the actions of men results in science and thought taking a contemplative form. The notion that the economic, social and historical process is independent of and uninfluenced by human activity is the precondition of its "calculability". The conditions of this process are studied and examined as if they were phenomena which obeyed supra-historical laws that man can then apply and use for his own benefit. The possibility that man's own actions actually change these laws is ignored. With natural science as its prototype, an exact science arises which looks contemplatively at the movement of the object from which it has detached itself, and tries to draw conclusive evidence from an insulated, empirical collection of facts.

Even more importantly, the view of the totality is lost. The social division of labour creates a series of special sub-spheres, not only in the economy but in the whole of social life and thought. These develop their own autonomous sets of laws. As a result of specialisation, each individual sphere develops according to the logic of its own specific object. The totality of sciences is not perceived as the total expression of social relations in their particular forms; on the contrary, individual spheres of knowledge become increasingly autonomous. Engels, writing about law, says:

"As soon as the new division of labour which creates professional lawyers becomes necessary, another new and independent sphere is opened up which, for all its general dependence on production and trade, still has its own capacity for reacting upon these spheres as well. . . . And the faithful reflection of economic relations is thereby more and more interfered with."[34]

What Engels says here about jurisprudence can be applied to science as a whole. The loss of the living relationship to the whole results in every individual sphere of knowledge tending to become a system in itself, extending and generalising its own problematic. Consequently the individual science, from its own standpoint and with its own method, tries to embrace all the other spheres and bring about the unity of knowledge by extending its own sphere. This, for example, is what lies behind Stammler's attempt to use the specific methods of jurisprudence to comprehend social processes. It is also typical of, for example, the various attempts at a "psychoanalytic" theory of the state.

But this exclusion of individual disciplines from the totality has a further consequence, which is that their own premises become transcendental and incomprehensible to themselves. In the end, they cannot understand either the method or the principle of even their own concrete substratum of reality. Marx was making a similar point on the subject of economics when he said that "use-value, as use-value, lies beyond the realm of consideration of political economy". The same is clearly true of jurisprudence. The prevailing positivist doctrine not only regards justice as a meta-legal concept, it also sees the connection between individual laws as a purely formal one. Kelsen poses this with particular clarity in his statement that "the content of legal institutions is never of a juridical character, but always political and economic"; the science of law is thus excluded from the content of law.

Similarly, philosophy is excluded from the concrete substrata of the individual sciences, since it takes results and methods of the individual sciences as given and necessary, reserving for itself the mere job of "uncovering and justifying the validity of the concepts thus formed", instead of "breaking through the barriers of this formalism which has fallen into isolated pieces, by means of a radically different orientation of the problematic, an orientation towards the concrete, material totality of what can and should be known. Philosophy in this case would be adopting the same position towards individual sciences as the latter in fact adopt towards empirical reality."[35]

Positivism and empiricism are characteristic of reified

thought. The "facts" are torn out of their total context and reappear as the object of knowledge in their own right. This kind of thought is basically analytic: it divides up the diversity of the totality and develops the individual parts. The connections between the individual parts and the relation of the parts to the whole are lost. The totality is no longer a unity, it remains merely the sum of individual spheres of knowledge. The "philosophical encyclopaedia" (e.g. Wundt) is an attempt to build this kind of "unity". The process is not restricted to the relation of individual sciences to each other; it also occurs within each science itself. Each one is increasingly broken down into individual sub-spheres. This phenomenon of specialisation, which occurs in all the sciences to the detriment of the total view, can be superficially verified by the increase in the number of manuals and technical dictionaries for each individual science, in place of thoroughgoing expositions of that science.

The loss of the totality of knowledge means that the real movement of reality cannot be adequately grasped. The individual moments of social life assume the form of isolated facts, of independent things, which only reassemble in reflection. Consequently they appear to be supra-historical entities; they are seen in a rigidified form instead of in flux. They lose their place in the social whole and are seen as isolated data, in objectified form, and not as relations in change: in hegelian language, they are seen as Substance, not as Subject. Marx, by contrast, demands that reality should be regarded neither as Object nor as contemplation, but as human, sensuous activity, and that it should be revolutionised by practical-critical activity. Only the application of the category of the concrete totality makes this possible. But the essence of the reified structure of thought is precisely the absence of such a mode of thinking: it is this reified structure which produces a false consciousness — ideology.

CHAPTER V: Ideology

Ideology and the Concept of the Concrete Totality

According to Engels, "ideology is a process accomplished by the so-called thinker consciously, no doubt, but with a false consciousness". Engels's description is the point of departure for the problem of ideology. Ideology means, first of all, a false consciousness which is not in accord with reality, which neither discovers nor expresses reality in an adequate manner. This, of course, raises the problem of what "reality" actually is, or to be more precise, what the materialist conception of history understands by "reality". Before we can answer this question, it is necessary to state that the marxist concept of ideology is a "total" one. Karl Mannheim's presentation of the concept of ideology supposes that thought is ideological in its very nature; on this basis, he distinguishes between a "partial" and a "total" concept of ideology.[36] In both cases, the examination of an opponent's ideas and the attempt to prove their falsity is made not on the direct basis merely of what the opponent states, but by way of an understanding of the holder of the ideas himself. Both approaches see the basis of false ideas as the location in being of those who hold them.

But with the partial concept of ideology, only a part of the opponent's ideas is examined, and its content disparaged as mere ideology. The examiner occupies the same theoretical ground as his opponent, since he is attempting to account for the opponent's ideas in psychological terms: his main theoretical framework is therefore a partial one, a psychology of interests, in which the opponent's ideas are demonstrated to be false on the grounds that they represent particular interests which force him to lie or, consciously or unconsciously, to mystify a state of fact.

With the total concept of ideology, on the other hand, it is the whole *Weltanschauung* of the opponent, including his methodology, which is called in question. Accordingly, the

98

holders of ideas and their social situation are not "functionalised" in mere psychological terms; their whole world of ideas is ascribed to their location in being. With the total concept of ideology, one seeks to discover the objective structural connections of the whole of the opponent's standpoint and approach.

The historical materialist concept of ideology is the "total" one. Consciousness is conscious being, and is determined by social being. A false consciousness must therefore correspond to a particular social situation, to a position in society from which correct knowledge is impossible. Ideas are, however, "correct" in the extent to which they are the adequate expression of their own particular social position; but at the same time, the objective falsity of consciousness is expressed by this very particularity. There is a particular kind of "illumination" or ideology for every social position. And since every social position in bourgeois society appears to be a partial one, all the knowledge and thought corresponding to each of these social positions must be regarded as ideology. As long as there is no deeper analysis of each social position, the ideologies which correspond to them appear, in principle, to be equivalent. Each particular set of ideas is capable of illuminating areas which remain concealed from other sets of ideas; all the partial aspects complement each other.

According to Max Weber, "the materialist conception of history is not some kind of taxi, which one can get into or out of at will; once inside, even the revolutionaries themselves are not free to leave it". Mannheim, too, correctly demands that the method of historical materialism be applied to historical materialism itself. According to him, historical materialism turns out to be an ideology corresponding to a "partial" social position, the ideology of the proletariat. The total concept of ideology, on the other hand, is a kind of "relationism", i.e. a sociology of knowledge which is concerned with the dependence of thought on being. Every historical and social position, including that of the proletariat, seems to be a partial one.

It is at this point that the difficulties begin to arise. The partial "correctness" of individual structures of consciousness has to be analysed in detail and given a proper evaluation. All

99

that Mannheim does is to remark that "a consciousness is false and ideological when it has not yet oriented itself towards an understanding of the new reality and therefore masks it with superseded categories", or, alternatively, when it has itself superseded being in the form of "utopian" consciousness. It is true that by this definition reality is seen as dynamic, as historically and socially transformable. But in practice it is too general a formula. Mannheim awards a partial but not purely subjective correctness to every partial standpoint. Consequently, when he comes to apply his thesis to the problem of the relation between theory and practice, he credits all the currents with which he deals (conservatism, bourgeois-democratic liberalism, socialism, fascism) with a certain correctness, but does not completely accept any one of them. This is supposed to demonstrate "the mutual and complementary nature of partial knowledges which are socially and politically linked".

This shows how far Mannheim has deviated from historical materialism. His interpretation and application of this most consistent of theories is thoroughly inconsistent. His mistake springs largely from the fact that he regards the individual social positions as equivalent, without analysing them any further. Historical materialism, on the contrary, examines the individual positions in society — classes — for the possibility of a correct consciousness which goes beyond their location in being; in doing so, it recognises that the proletariat is fundamentally distinct from all the other classes in bourgeois society since it is, from the beginning, a (negative) totality, a kind of society outside bourgeois society. Hence its standpoint cannot be described as partial, nor its consciousness as ideological. Where other classes and layers are concerned, we can prove the ideological character of their consciousness by analysing the relationship of their ideas to reality. But if we are to make this proof concrete, we need to define our concept of reality (which in itself is basically no different from Mannheim's) in a more precise way than Mannheim, with the aid of the dialectic.

What is "reality" in the materialist conception of history? Above all, it is not what "sound common sense" or "every worst kind of metaphysician" (Engels) regards as real. That is to say, reality is not the so-called facts at the surface of bourgeois society, things in their isolation as they appear under capitalism. The essence of things and their mode of appearance do not directly coincide:

"The final form of economic relations as seen on their surface, in their real existence and consequently in the ideas by which the bearers and agents of these relations seek to understand them, is very much different from, and indeed quite the reverse of, their inner but concealed essential form and the concept corresponding to it."[37]

The apparent facts at the surface are products of the reified appearance of the capitalist mode of production. Knowing reality means tearing aside this reified covering and penetrating to the inner, essential form of the relations, distinguishing this from its surface form. At the same time, however, it means showing that these forms of appearance are those which the essential form *must* take. Exposing and explaining reification means penetrating to the essence through the appearance. It means demonstrating the categories and methods by which we can comprehend reality *as a whole*, both as the essential form *and* as the surface (which has its own real existence).

First of all, we must understand reality not as a "complex of achieved things but as a complex of processes, in which things that are apparently stable, no less than concepts, undergo an uninterrupted change of coming into being and passing away"[38]: i.e. reality in its historical transformation, "becoming" rather than "being". This gives us a concrete understanding of the concepts which express that reality, whereas the a-historical mode of thinking gives these concepts an abstract, general character. Marx, writing in *The Critique of Political Economy* about the concept of "production", said that "when we speak of production, we always mean a particular stage in social development. . . . 'Production in general' is an abstraction, but a reasonable one, as long as it really brings out what is common, fixes it, and spares us repetition". It is necessary to make a distinction between the features which are common to all stages of production and the special features of each epoch. (The mistake of "vulgar economy" is to overlook this distinction: it regards what are actually the phenomena of capitalism alone as "natural" and eternal.) With his historically concrete mode of thinking, Marx manages to critically overturn the philosophical and general concept of "civil society" which he encounters in Hegel and to view it concretely as the bourgeois society of capitalism, which has a historical origin and is transitory. The examination of facts in the context of their historical development and the transformation of things in process, represent the first breach in the reified appearance of the capitalist social order.

But a historical understanding of social relationships, of reality, is only possible if facts are brought out of the isolated position in which they appear to superficial consideration. Apparently isolated facts must be looked at in their relationship to the whole, if their supra-historical appearance is to be penetrated. "The relations of production of every society form a whole," said Marx, and the same is true of social being in general. We can only understand reality correctly if the individual facts of social life are seen as moments of the social totality. The isolation of facts is a mere product of reification, masking their essential form and their inner connections. The empiricist or positivist attempt to present facts in this isolated way and to link them only conceptually, without looking at their real association, is in fact thoroughly unscientific, in spite of that special meticulousness which seems to mark such theories. The "crude stupidity" of this kind of thinking, in Marx's words, resides in the fact that it "establishes chance relationships between things which belong organically together, and regards the connection between them as one of sheer reflection".

The whole is not the sum of the parts. The parts find their meaning only in their relationship to the whole, in their integration in the totality. The category of totality, however, does not in any way suppress the individual moments. It is not an undifferentiated unity in which concrete phenomena disappear. Only the *appearance* of the individual life of its members — men, things, spheres of knowledge — is destroyed. It is replaced by their dialectical and dynamic relationship to the whole, and by their relationship to each other within the framework of the whole. Marx gave a striking account of this as it concerns the economy in *The Critique of Political Economy*:

> "The result which we arrive at is not that production, distribution, exchange and consumption are identical, but that they all form members of a whole, distinctions within a unity. . . . Consequently, a particular form of production determines particular forms of consumption, distribution and exchange, and particular relations of these different moments to each other. . . . There is interaction between the different moments."

And he adds that "this is the case for every organic whole". It is precisely the individual phenomenon's "relation to the whole" which determines its objective form. For example, only the machine's fixed position within the total context of capitalist society turns it into capital, or the product into the commodity; these things have apparent characteristics which do not actually belong to their material form.

An orientation of knowledge towards the whole makes it possible to break through the appearance of things — their apparent characteristics and apparent movement — and to see beyond, to the relationships of men themselves to each other. It enables us to understand the alienation of labour and the fetish appearance of commodity production. Only then can we understand the inner laws of movement of human society, which means understanding them at the same time as the product of men themselves and of forces that spring from relationships between men but have escaped their control. The category of the concrete totality, as the central category of the dialectic, reveals the humanist character of marxism. It is the actual category of reality. It allows us to verify how far consciousness accords with that reality, and how far it has an ideological character. Ideology is false, partial consciousness to the extent that it does not locate its object within the concrete totality, and thus to the exent that it is not adequate to the whole reality.

Ideology, however, is more than false consciousness. It is not a mere subjective fantasy but a "conscious" expression of the objective appearance assumed by capitalist reality. As conscious being, it is therefore an essential and necessary part of this reality. Ideology is the concept which corresponds to the real existence of the surface, as opposed to the correct, total consciousness which sees beyond the surface to the essential form of social relations. The reality of bourgeois society is made up not only of material relations but also of ideology.

The ideologies of capitalist society correspond to an economic base which rips apart the organic, turns men into things and the product of human labour into an acting subject. The notion that individual spheres of thought and knowledge are independent of each other and of their socio-economic base is ideological. The separation of consciousness from its object and the rupture of the unity between consciousness and being is ideological. Purely contemplative knowledge is ideological. But the whole superstructure of human ideas, too, is ideological, as long as these ideas maintain an apparent independence of the political and legal superstructure and of the economic base. And it is precisely this apparent autonomy of the superstructure which is the most important form of ideology. Ideological "sentiments, illusions, modes of thought and views of life", apparently detached from their material foundations, are not just subjective motivations for the actions of the individual man; they also correspond, objectively, to his social being. In Marx's words, "the individual who receives them through tradition and upbringing may imagine that they form the real motive and point of departure of his own activity". The superstructure of bourgeois society would therefore seem to be ideological, even in the narrowest sense of the word. But ideology is not an abstract fantasy. It is a part of the social reality of capitalism which marxism seeks not only to criticise theoretically but also to overthrow concretely, in practice.

Ideology and the Classes of Bourgeois Society

Ideology as false, partial consciousness corresponds to a particular position in society from which a correct, total understanding is impossible. We must therefore examine each individual social position within bourgeois society, to see how far it permits a correct, total view, and how far it leads to ideology. It is not a question of examining the social position of random individuals or groups, but of looking at those which, according to the materialist conception of history, are decisive, because they are distinguished essentially by their situation in the production process: i.e. classes. Ideology is a "conscious" expression of the objective, reified appearance of capitalism; the category of the concrete totality, on the other hand, is the concept which makes it possible to breach this reified appearance. The question now is to define more precisely what the possibilities are for any individual class to grasp the phenomenon of reification, to break through it and arrive at a concrete, total view.

I shall not deal here with the ideologies of the precapitalist epoch. A few basic distinctions between these periods and the period of capitalism will suffice. Capitalism and earlier social systems may all be described as having grown naturally, since they are the result of the most diverse voluntaristic impulses of men. Their impulses find an involuntary expression in these systems, but the latter are not the product of an overall, united organising will. In all these forms of production, human forces are objectified and turned into alien forces which dominate their possessors. Under precapitalist relations, however, the "natural" appearance of these forces is much greater, since real natural factors do actually play a much bigger and more direct role, and man's direct dependence on them (for example, on the harvest) is much greater and more obvious than under capitalism.

The fundamental significance of human and economic relationships only emerges fully when commodity production becomes general. Here for the first time, the general correlation between the individual parts of social life becomes explicit, whereas in all previous forms of production the parts are largely independent of the social whole. In precapitalist relations of production, some individual parts of society are autarchic and almost completely unconnected to the state, which is the general expression of the society; other parts, on the other hand, are economically parasitic and only exist through the state apparatus. It is only the general circulation of commodities, production for the market instead of for individual needs, that creates the general social context whose highest expression is the world market. Class relationships, too, first appear in a clear form in this capitalist context, whereas previously they had been concealed as estates, castes and other social groupings which grew and consolidated as a result of legal and state privileges. Since basic, verifiable economic states of fact still do not exist in clear form in these earlier forms of production, they cannot always be exactly "expressed" in legal or religious categories; rather, the latter are intertwined with them. Marx uses the example of the identity between rent and tax in the Asiatic mode of production, where ground rent is obtained by sheer force — the level of rent is not economically determined, and consequently there is no need for any separate form of taxation.

It is only under capitalism that the economy emerges as the foundation of social relationships. Of course, this was the case before the emergence of capitalism, and those social layers which appeared not to have been determined by the economy were in fact simply the rigidified forms of relations of production which had developed organically. Nevertheless, it is only under capitalism that there is a "pure" economy. Capitalism is a form of production which constantly reproduces itself on an enlarged scale, which continually revolutionises its own technology; in short, it is clearly dynamic in character, whereas the development of the precapitalist social forms proceeded extremely slowly, with the appearance of being almost static. Just as the social character of man's being only achieves expression under capitalism, so the historical evolution of existence and social institutions and concepts cease to assume a supra-historical significance. The "natural", non-human appearance of reality is thus far stronger and more opaque in all precapitalist relations of production than it is under capitalism, and its consciousness is much more ideological than bourgeois consciousness.

Bourgeoisie and proletariat are the main classes in bourgeois society. However, several very important layers — peasantry, petty bourgeoisie, etc. — overlap with the two decisive classes.

Let us deal with these layers first.

The middle classes are distinct from the two main classes of bourgeois society to the extent that they are less closely linked with the capitalist production process than the other two. Either their existence is indissolubly linked with the remnants of feudal society and their only association with the capitalist economy is an external one (peasants, artisans); or their role in economic life is restricted to the sphere of circulation (small businessmen, etc.); or else they are not direct participants in the economic process (liberal professions). They only come into contact with the basic phenomenon of capitalism, the commodity, when it is in circulation; or, if they actually manufacture commodities, then the form of manufacture is only partly capitalist, and is still associated with the production of goods for their own individual needs. Therefore none of them, from such a standpoint, can see through the fetish to the real character of commodities. Of course, the middle classes are in a position to see the symptoms of capitalism, but they cannot see the cause of these symptoms. Consequently, the economic and social changes which they strive for relate to the symptoms alone, and the changes, if achieved, remain within the framework of capitalism.

Because their situation in the production process does not allow them to recognise reification, human self-alienation, they regard history as a process which is determined directly by nature. A clear example of this is the appeal to biological factors as historically decisive (racial theories). The complementary aspect of this is their notion, likewise basically irrational, that history is the product of great individuals, regardless of the social circumstances. Fatalism (in this case naturalist, materialist fatalism) and subjectivism are the opposite sides of the same coin.

The middle classes are in a position to perceive the whole, but they cannot perceive it in its concrete diversity. They fail to see that the class antagonism between bourgeoisie and proletariat is decisive. What Marx wrote about the petty bourgeois democrats of his time can still be said to be true of the present-day political theories of the petty bourgeoisie (which proves the correctness of his judgment):

107

"But the democrat, because he represents the petty bourgeoisie, that is, a transitional class, in which the interests of two classes are simultaneously mutually blunted, imagines himself elevated above class antagonism generally. The democrats concede that a privileged class confronts them, but they, along with all the rest of the nation, form the people. What they represent is the people's rights; what interests them is the people's interests. . . . The peculiar character of social democracy is epitomised in the fact that democratic-republican institutions are demanded as a means, not of doing away with two extremes, capital and wage labour, but of weakening their antagonism and transforming it into harmony. However different the means proposed for the attainment of this end may be, however much it may be trimmed with more or less revolutionary notions, the content remains the same. This content is the transformation of society in a democratic way, but a transformation within the bounds of the petty bourgeoisie. . . . The petty bourgeoisie . . . believes . . . that the special conditions of its emancipation are the general conditions within the framework of which alone modern society can be saved and the class struggle avoided."[39]

Clearly, the layers which are not affected by this central problem of capitalist society must have false, partial conceptions. These may be subjectively correct, inasmuch as they are adequate to their individual situation, but they are objectively false, since they do not look at reality in its concrete wholeness. This means that their consciousness fails to achieve the goals of their own designation; at the same time, they achieve objective goals of social development which are unknown to them. The political practice of the petty bourgeoisie makes this clear. It involuntarily serves now one, now the other main class, according to the historical situation.

The question of whether the bourgeoisie itself, from its own particular social situation, is able to achieve a correct, non-ideological consciousness is actually answered by the manner in which the question is posed. We have seen that ideology is the expression of reification, at the level of consciousness. Reification is the central phenomenon of the entire life and thought of "bourgeois" society (i.e. society dominated by the bourgeoisie). Bourgeois consciousness, which is reified, is either the consciousness of the bourgeoisie or the bourgeois-dominated consciousness of other layers ("the dominant ideas of a period are always the ideas of the dominant class"). A correct consciousness, i.e. the recognition and breaking up of reification, is obviously not possible from this standpoint.

The bourgeois view, however, must be looked at from another angle. The bourgeoisie is in a dilemma. Even before it can fully overcome its feudal opponents and remove all trace of them, a new opponent is already confronting it, threatening its domination and seeking to overthrow the bourgeois social order. This opponent is the proletariat. Even before the bourgeoisie can fulfil its own revolutionary tasks, it grows conservative in face of the proletariat. A theoretical expression of this dilemma, this threat to its interests, can be found in the fact that whereas the first bourgeois historians demonstrated the real importance of the class struggle, they were followed by others who try to play it down or to reinterpret it as a struggle for class harmony. The classical students of early bourgeois political economy recognised the facts of the class struggle, but they were replaced by writers whom Marx labels "the apologists" because their theory is oriented towards the defence of capitalism and its so-called harmony.

The bourgeoisie were the first to recognise the economy as a total process, operating under a unified set of laws. It was capitalism which had brought about this unity and created a coherent society, in contrast to the particularity of all earlier social orders. But these laws appear to the bourgeoisie to be natural laws, which depend on the lack of consciousness of their participants. If the bourgeoisie were to recognise these laws as social and historical, this would obviously mean that it would also have to recognise its own domination as historically limited. Class interest and class consciousness thus contradict each other.

But this fact alone cannot account for the ideological nature of the consciousness which springs from the social position of the bourgeoisie. There is a much more decisive contradiction, which is that between social production and private appropriation. The means of production are produced socially and for society, but are in the hands of individual capitalists. "Capital is not a personal but a social power", but the movements of this power are directed by the individual interests of the owners of capital, who do not have an overall view of the social role of their activity. The laws and the social function of capital proceed, but "only over their heads, only irrespective of their will, without their consciousness." Private ownership of the means of production means that the only possible view from the position of the bourgeoisie is that of the individual capitalist; and to the individual capitalist, the laws which result from the alienation of labour must appear to be independent of man.

The bourgeoisie is as much subject to self-alienation as the proletariat, "but the possessing class . . . feels at home in this self-alienation, it finds confirmation of itself and recognises in alienation *its own power*". Unlike the proletariat, the bourgeoisie has no interest in seeing through and beyond this self-alienation or in removing it. The proletariat, however, is "annihilated" by it, lives an "inhuman existence" and is therefore forced to do everything in its power to remove it, theoretically and practically. From the point of view of the bourgeoisie, a knowledge of the *historical* character of bourgeois society is impossible. In addition, their particular standpoint corresponds to the isolated position of the capitalist, which makes a view of the totality impossible, and this isolation encourages partial knowledge of each separate, apparently autonomous sphere. Rationalisation and specialisation in the capitalist enterprise carry over into bourgeois knowledge and science. For all its enormous progress in individual spheres of knowledge, it fails to acquire a total vision, remaining partial and ideological:

> "If it is a work of science to resolve the visible, merely external movement into the true intrinsic movement, it is self-evident that conceptions which arise about the laws of production in the minds of agents of capitalist production and circulation will diverge drastically from

110

these real laws and will merely be the conscious expression of the visible movements. The conceptions of the merchant, stockbroker and banker, are quite necessarily distorted. Those of the manufacturers are vitiated by the acts of circulation to which their capital is subject, and by the levelling of the general rate of profit."[40]

The removal of reification is only possible from the standpoint of a class which, by its very conditions of life, is forced to prevent its individual members from being isolated and to bring them together consciously. Its consciousness already proceeds from a totality. The only class that can remove self-alienation is the class forced to do so by its conditions of existence, which are so deeply affected by the alienation of labour that the members of that class have themselves become commodities. Conversely, the fetish appearance of the commodity can only be removed when the commodity itself has become subject. The proletariat is the class which needs a correct consciousness of its situation in order to free itself and fulfil its historical role.

CHAPTER VI: Proletarian Class Consciousness

The Proletariat as Subject-Object in Capitalism

Reality is the same for bourgeoisie and proletariat. Both classes are subject to the same self-alienation. Reification applies to both. The question is whether the different social situation of the proletariat within the same capitalist reality allows it a different knowledge from the bourgeoisie's, and whether it is possible from this standpoint to break through reification and arrive at a total — and therefore no longer ideological — picture of reality.

The first striking distinction between bourgeoisie and proletariat is their difference of interests concerning the recognition and removal of self-alienation. Whereas the bourgeoisie feels at home and recognises "its own power" in self-alienation, and therefore has no interest in its removal, alienation for the proletariat represents an "inhuman existence". It is "driven directly to revolt against that inhumanity, through urgent, no longer disguisable, absolutely imperative need, that practical expression of necessity". A precondition for changing this situation is, however, the knowledge that it *can* be changed, the knowledge that social and economic laws are not natural laws independent of human action, but simply express the fact that the working man is separated from the product of his labour, which has become alien to him. Only this insight can help to eliminate the separation of the producer from the means of production and give man control over his own powers, which in the economy confront him as things. The dissolution of the reified appearance of reality and the removal of its material foundations are in the proletariat's own vital interests.

Private ownership of the means of production isolates the members of the bourgeoisie. Individual capitalists confront each other as independent, isolated possessors of commodities.

112

The point of departure for bourgeois consciousness is thus the individual man, the individual commodity-owner, the individual legal subject. The proletarians, in contrast, are massed together socially in the labour process:

> "At first the contest is carried on by individual workers, then by the workers of a factory, then by the workers of a trade, in one locality, against the individual bourgeois who directly exploits them. . . . But with the development of industry the proletariat not only increases in number, it becomes concentrated in greater masses. . . . The clashes between individual workers and individual bourgeois increasingly take on the character of clashes between the two classes. . ."[41]

The proletarians are forced into unity by their conditions of life. Their economic situation, first of all, unites them into a class confronting capital, a class "in itself", and the consciousness of this fact then makes it into a class "for itself". The point of departure for the proletarian is thus not individual man as such, but men as part of a whole, i.e. the class. From the beginning, then, proletarian consciousness proceeds from a totality. It thus breaks down one of the foremost limitations of bourgeois consciousness and recognises the basic fact about the economy, which is that it concerns relationships between the classes. At this point too, the specific legal mask worn by social relations under capitalism, by which individual subjects are equal under the law, becomes transparent.

But what is this class totality from which proletarian consciousness proceeds? It is not just a partial totality *within* bourgeois society, a class in the same sense that the bourgeoisie or the peasantry are classes. The proletariat is the negative totality of bourgeois society. "The abstraction of all humanity, even of the *semblance* of humanity, is practically complete" in the proletariat, "since the conditions of life of the proletariat sum up all the conditions of life of society today in all their inhuman acuity". The proletariat is so deeply affected by reification that its individual members have to sell themselves as commodities. Even "the appearance of humanity" is lost to the worker in the labour process; he has become a thing, a mechanical part, an appendage of the machine.

113

Thus, in a sense, the proletariat already stands outside bourgeois society. It is the negation of bourgeois society within that society itself. "By announcing the dissolution of the previous world order, the proletariat is simply revealing the secret of its own existence, for it is the dissolution in fact of that world order." It is precisely the proletarian's situation, in which he is furthest removed from "man", that enables him to know bourgeois society. Man himself is lost, but at the same time he has acquired the theoretical consciousness of this loss. Self-alienation has reached its highest stage. It abruptly turns into *recognition* of the alienated being of man, thus transcending itself [*sich aufheben*] in theory just as the proletariat removes [*aufheben*] it in practice, by means of revolutionary action. This practical removal of alienation consists of the proletariat's fight for political power and its use of political power to suppress private ownership of the means of production; this makes all men propertyless, like itself, and at the same time turns everyone into property-owners because the means of production are socialised. Society gains control over its own forces and now rules over them instead of being ruled by them.

The worker, as a commodity, has become Object, completely. He is totally subjugated to the social relations. His knowledge is the commodity's self-knowledge; his consciousness is the commodity's consciousness of itself. But there is also a relation of dialectical tension between the worker as man (i.e. outside the production process) and the worker as commodity-form in capitalist production. He appears to be able to separate his labour power from himself, in order to sell it. He sells this labour power as a legal subject, but in fact he is also selling himself, as a commodity. It is this separation between the objectivity and subjectivity of man in the process of becoming objectified as commodity, that enables him at the same time to become conscious of this situation. It means that the worker can only become conscious of his social being by becoming conscious of himself as a commodity.

The worker's knowledge of himself as a commodity is not, however, something which stops short at the immediate, reified objective appearance of capitalist reality. On the contrary, it is already mediated and penetrates through to the essential form

114

of this reality. This is because of the split, the dialectical tension between the subjectivity and objectivity of the worker, his dual role as commodity and as man. For the proletarian as *commodity*, a change in the number of his working hours is merely a quantitative change in his expenditure of labour power. But for the working *man*, it is a qualitative change, a change in the shape of his life. The proletarian as object, as the commodity labour-power, enters into a reified relationship with capital, but the essential form behind this objective appearance is a human relationship between the worker and the capitalist. The essential form is not, of course, a direct relationship between individuals but a social relationship mediated by the labour relation. Because the proletarian experiences this relationship both as object and subject, he is in a position to see through the fetish appearance of the commodity labour power. The worker can see that value is not an organic, inherent attribute of the commodity labour power, for he knows that this commodity is at the same time man, a legal subject who, outside production, is judged not by his material value but as the equal of all other men.

The "value" of the commodity labour power thus turns out to be a social relation. Once the fetish character of a commodity is seen through, it completely loses its mystery. The reified appearance is now recognised to be the surface of human, social relations. The proletariat thus occupies a position in society from which its consciousness can go beyond the appearances inherent in the immediacy of fact and orient itself towards the whole.

To the proletarian who is simultaneously thing and man, object and subject, reality reveals that it too has a dual character: it is both essence and appearance, it is both the inner, essential form and the surface. The proletarian's experience of this situation enables him, proceeding from the achieved form of reification, to know the whole of social reality as essence and appearance. Self-alienation has reached its peak in the proletariat. By becoming object, thing, man has at the same time become the subject and object of knowledge. This is what "the self-knowledge of reality" means, in the dialectical materialist sense. In the process of man's becoming a thing, the reified structure of reality dissolves and becomes human and social. The fact that man and thing have become one, without man ceasing to be consciously man, reveals the human character of relationships between things.

Class Ideology and Class Consciousness

To state that the proletariat's position in society allows it a correct, non-ideological consciousness, a non-reified knowledge of reality in its concrete totality, does not mean that the proletariat actually has such a consciousness. A non-reified, proletarian class consciousness must also recognise the theoretical conclusions which Marx and Engels came to, on the basis of the following steps:

1. The class struggle and its socio-economic foundations.
2. The historical and transitory character of capitalism.
3. Capitalism supplying the lever for its own defeat, in the shape of the proletariat.
4. The proletariat's distinction from all other revolutionary classes in that its rule does not lead to a new form of exploitation; it can only free itself by freeing the whole of society at the same time.
5. The proletariat's use of its own class rule to socialise the means of production so that classes actually disappear (and with them the state, the expression of class struggle).

In other words, a correct proletarian class consciousness must reach the conclusion that in fighting for and exercising political power, the proletariat can remove the foundations of human self-alienation and in so doing dissolve itself as a class. Obviously, however, this kind of consciousness does not currently prevail among the proletariat or even a major part of it in any country, apart from the Soviet Union. This developed form of proletarian class consciousness is therefore not an actual consciousness but an imputed [*zugerechnet*] one, a consciousness which the proletariat would have if it were capable of fully comprehending its situation. This imputed class consciousness is not something that is completely independent of

116

the real consciousness of individual members of the proletariat. The former is what Marx called socialist or communist consciousness; the latter is class ideology or class experience.

Let us examine the relation between the two more closely. Because the working class suffers from self-alienation and therefore from reification, it is still as a whole incapable of a correct, non-ideological consciousness. Yet only the removal of human self-alienation can bring it to a socialist consciousness. In this context, Marx wrote:

> "For the production on a mass scale of this communist consciousness . . . the transformation of men on a mass scale is necessary, and this can only take place in a practical movement, a revolution; this revolution is necessary, therefore, not only because the ruling class cannot be overthrown in any other way, but because, too, the class overthrowing it can only in a revolution succeed in getting rid of all the filth of past ages . . ."[42]

Only revolution, the actual removal of reification, can make the communist consciousness general. Once this happens, it is no longer class consciousness but human consciousness.

But it is already possible in bourgeois society to see through the reified appearance. The humanist, dialectical materialist theory represents non-reified knowledge. It anticipates what the proletariat as a whole can only know after its liberation. It is therefore an anticipatory class consciousness, which is indispensable to the unity of theory and practice that is the precondition for the victory of the proletariat. For the proletariat, correct consciousness is the necessary condition of correct action; "practice" does not mean unconscious activity but forms a unity with the concept of that practice. Lenin expressed this well when he said that "without revolutionary theory there can be no revolutionary movement".

Correct consciousness does not in the least coincide with the ideology of the proletariat: "the question is not what goal is envisaged for the time being by this or that member of the proletariat, or even by the proletariat as a whole; the question is, what *is* the proletariat and what course of action will it be forced historically to take in conformity with its own nature?"[43] The kind of consciousness which is a constituent part of this historically necessary action achieves expression in socialist theory.

This may seem to imply that the working-class movement and marxist theory develop independently of each other and only connect externally. The proletariat needs a correct consciousness in order to win, but it does not acquire this consciousness by itself, although from its point of view such a consciousness is possible. Marxist theory, on the other hand, is a correct consciousness, but its origins lie outside the working-class movement, in the minds of intellectuals. Hence, in the line of reasoning followed by both Lenin and Kautsky, marxist theory has to be introduced into the workers' movement from outside. In the debate on a draft programme for Austrian social democracy, Kautsky wrote:

"Socialism as a doctrine is as deeply rooted in present-day economic relations as the class struggle of the proletariat. . . . But the two things sprang up under different conditions and alongside each other, not out of each other. Modern socialist consciousness can only arise on the basis of deep scientific insight. . . . The bearer of science, however, is not the proletariat but the bourgeois intelligentsia; modern socialism therefore originates from individual members of this layer, and it is communicated by them only to intellectually outstanding proletarians, who then introduce it into the class struggle of the proletariat, where conditions allow. Socialist consciousness is thus something introduced into the proletarian class struggle, not something which is born 'naturally' from it."

Lenin develops these "very striking and significant" ideas of Kautsky in detail, in *What Is To Be Done?*:

"We have said that the workers *could not yet have* a social democratic consciousness. This consciousness could only be brought to them from outside. The history of all countries shows that the working class, exclusively by its own effort, is able to develop only trade union consciousness, i.e. it may itself realise the necessity for combining in unions, for fighting against the employers and for striving to compel the government to pass necessary labour legislation etc. . . . The theory of socialism, how-

118

ever, grew out of the philosophical, historical and economic theories that were elaborated by the educated representatives of the propertied classes, the intellectuals."

But this raises certain questions. If socialist theory is introduced into the workers' movement from outside, why then does it have to be *socialist* theory which the proletariat chooses to adopt? It might be any other theory — a fascist, liberal or conservative one, in which case the proletariat, for lack of a correct, non-ideological consciousness, would not win the victory which marxism proposes for it. Both these "orthodox marxists", Lenin and Kautsky, deviate considerably here from Marx's conception of the relation between theory and the workers' movement. In *The Communist Manifesto* he clearly describes theory as the general expression of the class struggle, of a historical movement.

Lenin and Kautsky rupture the marxist unity of theory and practice. In reality, the relation between theory and the working-class movement is much tighter than they suppose. Theory does not only enter into association with the movement from outside, it is also the necessary expression of that movement: "it is not enough that thought tends to become reality, but also that reality tends to become thought".

Lenin's conception of the spontaneous origins of proletarian consciousness is incomplete. According to Lenin, the proletariat by itself only develops a trade-union, reformist consciousness, which enables it to recognise the need to improve its situation by means of its own activity, but only within the framework of the existing bourgeois social order; this kind of consciousness is thoroughly reified, sees only the "facts" on the surface and has a fatalistic view of the "natural laws" of the economy ("a crisis is not the time for struggle" — this well-worn trade union leaders' formula is a typical example of this attitude). But Lenin overlooks the other ideology which is also spontaneously produced by the proletariat: the ideology which aims at the revolutionary liberation of the working class at times when revolutionary action cannot be brought into line with the objective conditions. This tendency has nothing at all to do with the day-to-day struggle of the workers: it is concerned exclusively with the revolutionary goal and with revolutionary

119

action, either by the masses or by a determined minority, regardless of the given socio-economic situation.

This utopian, subjectivist consciousness seeks to lift the future directly into the present, while the fatalistic, reformist consciousness sees present reality as everlasting. The two ideologies complement each other and are produced alongside each other by the working class. One is expressed by the trade unions and reformist parties. The other is expressed by anarchism. Both ideologies are a result of the quite contradictory situation of the proletariat, the contradiction between their day-to-day struggles within the framework of capitalism and their struggle for the overthrow of the whole capitalist order. This contradiction is at the root of the whole existence of the proletariat: in a real sense, the proletariat is both a constituent part of capitalism and its negation, its removal.

Marxism is the synthesis of both conceptions. It joins with the day-to-day struggle of the proletariat and demonstrates that at a certain point it must turn from a struggle within capitalism to a struggle against capitalism. Marxism does not regard evolution and revolution as opposites. The revolution is a moment in evolution. A quantitative growth in the struggles of the proletariat turns into a qualitatively new type of struggle. As long as it recognises this, marxist *theory* approaches very closely the *ideology* of the proletariat, since it is nothing but the fusion, at a higher stage, of both the above-mentioned tendencies of that ideology.

However, this also demonstrates clearly that theory is not introduced into the workers' movement arbitrarily. Marxist theory is only capable of taking hold of the masses because it is attached to the consciousness of the masses. The adoption of marxist theory by the working-class movement only follows because, and to the extent that, this theory allows the movement to become conscious of its own actions. The proletariat as a whole can only acquire this consciousness, in its totality and expressed by the theory, after the actual removal of reification. But a part of the class is able as a result of its own experiences to perceive the direction of the development, and therefore adopts the theory. This part, which consists of the most progressive, most "class conscious" elements of the proletariat, makes up the revolutionary party; it is now in a position to explain the actions of the working class to it and thereby orient it towards its goal.

This is how theory influences the working-class movement. Without it they remain separate. Of course, it cannot be denied that intellectuals founded and developed marxist theory. But Marx and Engels and their descendants could only do so from the standpoint of the proletariat and in close contact with the proletarian movement. Marx and Engels were the founders of the First International and "introduced" their theories into the workers' movement, but they could only work out these theories because there was already an existing proletarian movement for them to observe. Among the English chartists, the French blanquists and other similar groups they found not only a movement but also, from the beginning, the content of a consciousness to which their theory gave form and expression. Theory and the working-class movement, therefore, do not develop along parallel lines that only meet in an external sense; they form a unity of living interaction. The tendency of both socialist consciousness and class ideology is to approach each other until they reach the point where, following the removal of reification, they fuse.

Marxist theory does not only originate from those "philosophical, historical and economic theories" which in Lenin's words "were elaborated by the educated representatives of the propertied classes, the intellectuals". It is also the critique of these theories, the critique of bourgeois ideology, corresponding to the practical critique which the working class made of the economic foundations of this ideology. It is no accident that the foundations of this theory were laid down between 1843 and 1848, at a time when a revolutionary situation was already posing the task of the seizure of power to the young working-class movement. Theory, therefore, is not simply "rooted in economic relations". It is the expression of a real, historical movement. In Korsch's words, it is "the theory of social development seen and understood as living totality, or more precisely: the theory of social revolution understood and put into practice as living totality". Revolutionary practice and the

121

understanding of that practice form a unity.

Marx's "critical and revolutionary theory in its essence" is the expression of the critical and revolutionary practice of the working-class movement. On the other hand, the working-class movement can only adopt the theory as long as this corresponds to the movement's practice. When class antagonisms come to a head in revolutionary situations, it is easier for the proletariat to see through the surface reality than at other times. The goal of the struggle becomes clearer and more realistic than before, and both the reformist and the subjectivist ideologies lose ground before socialist consciousness, which is now given some muscle by class experience. In such situations the consciousness of the whole class develops in an extraordinarily short space of time, as a result of their accumulated experience. On the other hand, there are periods such as from 1850 to the turn of the century when the whole workers' movement, including that section which calls itself socialist or marxist, either did not adopt marxist theory at all or merely adopted a garbled version of it, which corresponded to the essentially non-revolutionary character of the workers' movement in that period.

Even the most enlightened and progressive part of the working class, the revolutionary party (the "vanguard", in Lenin's terms), can only adopt socialist consciousness and theory if these correspond to its practice and that of the class. The party cannot introduce socialist consciousness into the proletariat at any unspecified time, or under any circumstances. This, however, was Lenin's view of the party. He believed that the party must combat the spontaneism of the masses and implant socialist consciousness, and he regarded it as the actual producer of (correct) class consciousness. His standpoint and the principles of organisation that went with it were criticised by Rosa Luxemburg. She saw the party basically as the *product* of class consciousness and of the class movement, which only becomes clear about its tasks in the course of struggle. She emphasised the spontaneity of that struggle and the spontaneous character of working-class consciousness. But neither is this view fully correct. The party is not only the result of the class movement but can also intervene actively in it and

122

determine the direction it takes, by making the masses conscious of their own action. While the class as a whole recognises its tasks only in the course of struggle, a part of it, the party, already knows the direction from the experience of previous struggles. At these times it plays a vanguard role, and not only the conservative role which Rosa Luxemburg attributes to it:

> "The communists are, in a practical sense, the most determined section of the workers' parties in all countries, the section which drives on the rest; in a theoretical sense, they are ahead of the mass of the proletariat because they have an understanding of the conditions, progress and general results of the proletarian movement."[44]

The party is simultaneously the *product* and the *producer* of class consciousness. Lenin brings out only the one side, Luxemburg only the other. Naturally each of them speaks of the dialectical relation between party and class consciousness, and each points out the connection with the other side of this relation. Thus Luxemburg writes that the party should not wait with folded arms for the appearance of a revolutionary situation, but on the contrary should try to accelerate the development of events, by "making the widest possible sections of the proletariat understand the inevitability of the coming of this revolutionary period, the inner social conditions which are leading to it and the political consequences", in order to take the leadership of the movement in hand. Conversely Lenin, in *Left-Wing Communism: An Infantile Disorder* (1920), spoke emphatically of linking the party with the toiling masses, even of its fusing with them. Even so, neither Lenin nor Luxemburg makes a clear enough presentation of the dialectical unity of theory and the workers' movement, or of the interrelationship between socialist consciousness and practical-critical activity.

Marxism as Ideology and as Humanism

Throughout this work I have used the method of marxism to give an account of marxism, from the concept of dynamic,

123

social being to its interaction with the revolutionary practice of the proletariat. How, with the same method, can we account for the distortion of marxist theory by the epigones? Rosa Luxemburg referred to the phenomenon of "theoretical stagnation" as early as 1903 in an article in *Vorwärts* (14 March). Her explanation for this stagnation was that Marx's scientific work had overtaken the practical movement of the working class. This explanation, however, stands the relation between theory and practice on its head. In reality the high level which historical materialist theory reached in its founders is due to the fact that it was an expression of the similarly high practical level which the class struggle of the proletariat had already reached around 1848, with the upsurge in the whole revolutionary movement during that period. But whereas marxist theory continued after that to be founded on the experiences of 1848, the practical-critical activity of the proletariat fell back from this high level; the adoption of marxist theory by the workers' movement at the end of the nineteenth century was purely formal and ideological, and was not this time determined by a critical and revolutionary practice.

This produced the separation between theory and practice which took the practical character out of marxism and reduced it to "pure", contemplative, "objective scientific theory". Marxist theory was deprived of its critical and revolutionary meaning. The elimination of the dialectical unity between theory and practice expressed itself in theory as the destruction of the dialectical unity between consciousness and being; it turned Marx's doctrine into an aggregation of rigid formulae. The distortion of marxism by Kautsky and the other marxist epigones is a consequence of this.

The attempt to re-harmonise theory and practice comes from two tendencies in particular. One is revisionism, which tries to adapt theory to a non-revolutionary, essentially reformist practice; the Second International has been doing this since before the war, in spite of its repeated formal rejections of revisionist theory. Where revisionism does accept marxism it lays special emphasis on Marx's presentation of the laws of development, giving them a fatalistic interpretation. The second tendency is Lenin's, who as a practical revolutionary

124

tried to raise the practice of the workers' movement to the same level that the theory had achieved with its founders. This explains his idea that socialist consciousness must be introduced into the workers' movement from outside, and it explains his fight against spontaneity and his insistence on the leading role of the party. But this attempt to adjust practice to the level of theory obviously cannot be successful at any point in time, regardless of the objective situation. Until 1917 the separation between theory and practice continued to exist; this much was evident from Lenin's theory itself in that period, as we have already seen.

A real unity between the critical and revolutionary theory of marxism and the revolutionary practice of the workers' movement occurred between 1917 and 1923, and on a much broader scale than in Marx's time. This unity, and with it the restoration of the original meaning of marxist theory, appears at its clearest in Lenin's *State and Revolution*. Marx's theory of the conquest and exercise of power by the proletariat is renewed here, and it is closely connected with the revolutionary practice of the workers' movement at that time. This renewed harmony between theory and practice also affected the relation between the party, as bearers of the theory, and the working class. In 1920 Lenin demanded the fusion of the two, thus deviating considerably from what he had written in *What Is To Be Done?* Finally, the two works which recognise the crisis in marxist theory to the fullest extent and which restore the sense of Marx's own theory to the field of historical materialism — Lukács's *History and Class Consciousness* and Korsch's *Marxism and Philosophy* — are themselves products of that same period, and their authors had direct links with the revolutionary practice of the workers' movement.

In *Marxism and Philosophy*, Korsch distinguishes three phases in the development of the relation between marxism and the workers' movement. The first phase dates from the origins of marxist theory to the defeat of the 1848-49 revolutions. In this period, revolutionary theory was the expression of a corresponding practice. In the period following their defeat, which lasted till the end of the nineteenth century, the practice of the workers' movement began from a much

125

lower level; marxist theory developed independently of it. After the turn of the century a *rapprochement* took place. A revolutionary period was beginning, and the working-class movement strove for a level of practice which marxist theory could adequately express. Korsch's breakdown is useful as a rough approximation, although the periods are too long for any clear estimate of the importance of their individual concrete features.

The tendency towards the uniting of marxism with the workers' movement, and with it the restoration of the real sense of marxist theory, only became a reality in the 1917-23 period, in spite of the isolated individual attempts which had been taking place from the beginning of the century. The ebbing of the revolutionary movement of the proletariat since then has deepened the rift between theory and practice once again, and this has had distorting effects on the theory. The ideological character of marxism has been maintained by the theoreticians of the Second International such as Kautsky and Adler. It has appeared equally in the Third International, which by sticking so closely to Lenin's ideas of 1917 has actually deviated further than Lenin himself from Marx's and Engels's materialist conception of history. Max Raphael's book *Towards a Theory of Knowledge of the Concrete Dialectic* is an example. In it, he develops Lenin's metaphysical and naturalist materialism to absurd extremes, while in the same breath rejecting all other "pure", i.e. contemplative, theories of cognition as "metaphysics". He completely distorts the humanist character of the unity of consciousness and being. He refers to the unity of "matter and mind" and the "dialectical theory of reflection", defining the relation between consciousness and being as follows:

> "Where world and man confront each other [sic], it is (historically determined) existence which determines consciousness (whose origins are historical and social) and not the other way round, i.e. (human or absolute) consciousness does not determine (sensuous or abstract) being."

It would be superfluous to demonstrate in detail how Raphael distorts Marx's conception of the problem; we merely need to note the distance which separates this from the *Theses on Feuerbach* or *The German Ideology*. It is only one example of many which could be quoted from the literature of the Third International.

The various theories which currently describe themselves as "materialist conceptions of history" clearly diverge very sharply from each other and even more sharply from the theory of Marx and Engels. For historical materialism to live again and bear fruit, in its original humanist form, the working-class movement must again reach the level which it has reached before on a narrower base of capitalist development, and the theory must again be the adequate expression of that movement. According to the marxist conception the movement can and must reach this level if it is to fulfil its real task, the removal of human self-alienation. Practice will decide whether the humanist, materialist theory is true or false.

It is the basic humanist element in historical materialism which leads to recognition of the dialectical unity of consciousness and being, and which also explains why thought and the object of thought appear to be separate from each other. With the natural growth in the division of labour man's own forces become alien to him, and confront him from an independent position. With the development of capitalism in particular, the fetishism of the commodity occurs, and in reification it acquires a general character. But this also means that the expression of reification at the level of consciousness, i.e. ideology, becomes transparent: the proletariat, which is itself the product of capitalism, is in a position in society from which it is possible, by means of its practical-critical activity, to see through reification. Humanism signifies the self-knowledge of reality, which is also the self-knowledge of man: the self-knowledge of human, social being.

But humanism signifies more than this. Capitalism has freed man from direct domination by the factors of nature, and replaced this with domination by social and economic relationships, on the foundation of natural realities. These social and economic relationships are in actual fact man's own forces. They oppose him because of the alienation of labour, and they

127

are objectified as alien powers ruling over man. In creating the proletariat, capitalism has created a class which is forced by "need, the practical expression of necessity" to rise up against these relations and transform them. The liberation of the proletariat can only come about through the appropriation of the alienated social forces, i.e. the socialisation of the means of production, which will mean that self-alienation is removed and that the "human essence" will rediscover the "true reality" which it has lost:

> "The whole sphere of the conditions of life which surround man, and which have hitherto ruled man, now comes under the dominion and control of man, who for the first time becomes the real, conscious master of nature, because he has now become master of his own socialisation. The laws of his own social action, hitherto confronting man as laws of nature alien to him and dominating him, will then be used with full understanding and thus be mastered by him. Man's socialisation, which previously confronted him as something imposed from above by nature and history, now becomes his own free action. The alien objective forces which till now have dominated history, pass to the control of man himself."[45]

Humanism signifies the self-realisation of man. The rule of things over man is removed; society organises its own forces consciously, "in the realm of freedom".

Marxist humanism is therefore a radical critique of bourgeois ideology and of the material foundations of that ideology: it removes self-alienation in thought and in theory. But it is also both the means and the expression of a radical revolution in social relations, removing alienation in practice. "To be radical", according to Marx, "is to grasp things at the root: but for man, the root is man himself."

NOTES

1. Engels, "Anti-Dühring", in *Engels: Selected Writings* (London: Penguin Books, 1967), p.185.
2. Marx, Afterword to the second German edition of *Capital* (Moscow: Progress Publishers, 1963), vol. 1, pp.19-20.
3. See Engels, *Ludwig Feuerbach*.
4. Ludwig Woltmann, *Der historische Materialismus* (1900), p.114.
5. See Feuerbach, *Vorläufige Thesen zur Reform der Philosophie*.
6. *Ibid.*
7. Marx, Afterword to the second German edition of *Capital*, p.19.
8. Marx, *Economic and Philosophic Manuscripts of 1844* (Moscow: Progress Publishers, 1959), p.150.
9. Marx, *The German Ideology* (London: Lawrence and Wishart, 1970), p.63.
10. Marx, *Economic and Philosophic Manuscripts of 1844*, p.100.
11. Marx, *ibid.*, p.97.
12. Rudolf Stammler, *Wirtschaft und Recht nach der materialistischen Geschichtsauffassung* (3rd edition, 1914), p.280.
13. Marx, *The German Ideology*, p.63.
14. Engels, *The Origin of the Family, Private Property and the State* (New York: International Publishers, 1942), p.155.
15. *Ibid.*
16. Marx, *Capital*, vol. I, p.84.
17. E. B. Pashukanis, *La Théorie Générale du Droit et le Marxisme* (Paris: EDI, 1973), p.33.
18. Lenin, *Materialism and Empirio-Criticism* (Peking: Foreign Languages Press, 1972), p.394.
19. Lenin, *ibid.*, p.391.
20. See Alexander Deborin, *Lenin, der kämpfende Materialist* (1924).
21. See Max Adler, *Lehrbuch der materialistischen Geschichtsauffassung* (1930).
22. Marx and Engels, *The Holy Family* (Moscow: Progress Publishers, 1956), p.73.
23. See Karl Korsch, *Marxism and Philosophy* (London: New Left Books, 1970).

24. Marx, *Economic and Philosophic Manuscripts of 1844*, pp.66-7.
25. *Ibid.*
26. Marx, *Capital*, vol. III, p.831.
27. Marx and Engels, *The Holy Family*, p.51.
28. Marx, *Capital*, vol. I, p.72.
29. Marx, *The German Ideology*, pp.91-2.
30. Marx, *Capital*, vol. I, p.77.
31. Marx, *ibid.*, p.424.
32. Marx, *Capital*, vol. III, p.392.
33. See Max Weber, *Gesammelte politische Schriften*, pp.140-142.
34. Engels, Letter to Conrad Schmidt (27 October 1890).
35. Georg Lukács, *History and Class Consciousness* (London: Merlin Press, 1971), p.109.
36. See Karl Mannheim, *Ideology and Utopia* (London: Routledge and Kegan Paul, 1936).
37. Marx, *Capital*, vol. III, pp.208-209.
38. *Engels: Selected Writings* (see note 1), p.317.
39. Marx, *The Eighteenth Brumaire of Louis Bonaparte* (Moscow: Progress Publishers, 1954), p.40.
40. Marx, *Capital*, vol. III, p.313.
41. Marx and Engels, *The Communist Manifesto* (London: Penguin Books, 1967), pp.88-9.
42. Marx, *The German Ideology*, pp.94-5.
43. Marx and Engels, *The Holy Family*, p.53.
44. Marx and Engels, *The Communist Manifesto*, p.95.
45. *Engels: Selected Writings*, p.223.

INDEX OF NAMES

Adler, Max, 22, 23, 67, 68, 72-5, 77, 126;
Lehrbuch der material-
istischen Geschichtsauf-
fassung, 73

Belleville, Fritz, 7
Bernstein, Eduard, 67
Braunthal, Alfred, 67
Brinkmann, Carl, 56
Büchner, Ludwig, 27

Comte, Auguste, 22

Deborin, Alexandre, 72;
Lenin, der kämpfende
Materialist, 72
De Man, Hendrik, 55, 67;
Towards a Psychology of
Socialism, 55
Diderot, Denis, 71

Engels, Friedrich, passim;
Anti-Dühring, 13, 101;
letter to J. Bloch, 38;
letter to Mehring, 55;
letter to Conrad Schmidt, 49, 95;
Ludwig Feuerbach, 14, 16, 18;
The Origin of the Family,
Private Property and the
State, 41, 42.
See also under Marx

Feuerbach, Ludwig, 13-14, 16, 17-18, 20-7, 62, 66, 69, 70, 75;

The Essence of Christianity, 21;
History of the New Philo-
sophy, 21;
Philosophy of the Future, 14;
Vorläufige Thesen zur Reform
der Philosophie, 16-17
Fogarasi, 76
Fraenkel, Boris, 8
Franco, General, 7

Hegel, G.W.F., 13, 15-20, 21, 22, 24, 26, 28, 61, 66, 71, 72, 102;
Phenomenology of Mind, 71
Hilferding, Rudolf, 72;
Finance Capital, 63

Kant, Immanuel, 15
Kautsky, Karl, 64, 67, 68-70, 72, 73, 75, 76, 118, 119, 124, 126;
The Materialist Conception of
History, 68
Kelsen, Hans, 47, 50, 96
Korsch, Karl, 7, 68, 76ff., 121, 125, 126;
Marxism and Philosophy, 76, 77, 125;
The Materialist Conception of
History: A Debate with
Karl Kautsky, 76

Lenin, 13, 20, 67, 70-2, 73, 75, 78, 80, 118, 119, 121, 122ff.;
Left-Wing Communism: An
Infantile Disorder, 123;

131

State and Revolution, 125;
What Is To Be Done?, 118, 125
Lukács, Georg, 76, 78-80;
History and Class Consciousness, 78, 96, 125
Luppol, I., 72
Lutte Ouvrière, 8
Luxemburg, Rosa, 122-23, 124

Mannheim, Karl, 98, 99-100;
Ideology and Utopia, 98
Marx, Karl, *passim*;
Capital, 20, 46, 67, 86, 88, 89, 90, 92-4, 101, 110-11;
A Critique of Hegel's "Philosophy of Law", 24, 62;
A Critique of Political Economy (Grundrisse), 14, 30, 36, 38, 90, 101, 103;
Economic and Philosophical Manuscripts of 1844, 15, 27, 28, 29, 85, 86;
The Eighteenth Brumaire of Louis Bonaparte, 38, 108;
letter to Arnold Ruge, 14;
letter of J.B. Schweitzer, 21;
Theses on Feuerbach;
Marx and Engels, *The Communist Manifesto*, 75, 113, 119, 123;
The German Ideology, 15, 23, 24, 28, 31, 35, 37, 74, 89, 117, 127;
The Holy Family, 14, 15, 19, 20, 22, 57, 71, 74, 87, 117
Moleschott, 27
Münzer, Thomas, 54

Pashukanis, E.B., *La Théoric Générale du Droit et le Marxisme*, 51
Plekhanov, Georg, 34, 39, 54, 67

Raphael, Max, 126;
Towards a Theory of Knowledge of the Concrete Dialectic, 126
Reich, Wilhelm, 8
Révai, Joszef, 76
Rousseau, Jean-Jacques, 54
Rudas, Ladislaus, 79

Stammler, Rudolf, 33;
Wirtschaft und Recht nach der materialistischen Geschichtsauffassung, 33

Taylor (system), 91
Trotsky, Leon, 8

Vico, Giambattista, 64;
Principles of a New Science on the Nature of Peoples, 28-9
Vogt, 27
Vorländer, Karl, 67
Vorwärts, 124

Weber, Max, 94, 99;
Gesammelte politische Schriften, 94
Woltmann, Ludwig, 67;
Der historische Materialismus, 16
Wundt, 97